Enter the Ring is everything I've come to e[x...] and Elicia Horton—gritty, creative, hard h[...] centered, powerful, and life changing. This is a seriously great book—you'll laugh sometimes and feel like you got punched in the gut at other times (and in this book there's usually only seconds between the two, so when you're chuckling to yourself, watch out). In all of it, you'll find yourself looking upward to Jesus with amazement to find the hope and grace in your relationships that D. A. and Elicia have found in theirs.

J. D. GREEAR, PhD
Pastor, The Summit Church, Raleigh-Durham, North Carolina

Enter the Ring is an unveiling of the deep struggles involved in making a marriage work. In true millennial fashion, D. A. and Elicia Horton open up their lives before us so we can have front-row seats in seeing God work. This book will challenge readers from all generations to pursue gospel-saturated lifestyles that serve as an apologetic for our faith.

ED STETZER
Billy Graham Distinguished Chair, Wheaton College Graduate School

Enter the Ring is a book that considers the nuances of being unapologetically Christian, married, and urban. It's both refreshing and reassuring to see the raw realness of marriage expressed in these pages. The Hortons' vulnerability and practicability in their approach to marriage is a needed voice in the genre.

PROPAGANDA AND DR. ALMA
The Red Couch Podcast

Reading *Enter the Ring* makes you feel as though you're sitting in the Hortons' living room on their couch while they're talking to you about marriage. This book is relatable, transparent, and deeply convicting—and all the while it points you back to the One who is able to heal even the deepest of marital hurts. The Hortons remind us that while marriage can be difficult, the Redeemer is still able to make beauty from ashes.

RICK AND ROSIE HARRIS
The Summit Church, Raleigh-Durham, North Carolina

Enter the Ring is a gospel-saturated, practical, informational, and inspirational book on marriage. I love D. A. and Elicia's transparency about their personal struggles for oneness and for defining oneness biblically and relationally. The IDEAL acronym they define is great for handling conflict in a loving and healthy way, and hearing from both of them is helpful. From communication to sexual intimacy, this book covers the whole gamut of what marriage is, what it does, and the goal God has in bringing two people together. This is a great book no matter where you are on your marriage journey. I highly recommended this book for couples and for churches desiring to equip their couples for lasting marriages.

JEROME GAY JR.
Pastor, Vision Church, Raleigh, North Carolina

Just yesterday I received a request to pray for a marriage. After praying for this couple, I thought of *Enter the Ring*. D. A. and Elicia are writing to save marriages, and we need to save marriages now more than ever before. Practical and gospel based, this book is a godsend. As D. A. and Elicia write, "We can choose to fight for our marriages. And with God's help, we can win."

OSAZE MURRAY
Recording artist and African American Network director
with The Navigators

This is not your *Leave It to Beaver*, "high school sweethearts fall in love and live happily ever after" kind of marriage book. It's more like a "How in the world did these two end up getting married and staying together?" kind of marriage book. It's the kind of book that's needed in a self-absorbed, sex-crazed, anti-commitment world filled with brokenhearted singles and disillusioned young marrieds. With down-to-earth, street-level, blunt honesty, D. A. and Elicia Horton speak out of their own relational struggles and into the lives of anyone willing to listen regarding how to *Enter the Ring* and fight together for a gospel-saturated marriage. Take up and read this book in your single years, in premarital counseling, and in your first years of marriage. Watch as D. A. and Elicia demonstrate how the gospel is worked out in marriage. Let them walk you through the practical ways of fighting *together*, rather than against each other, in various potential areas of conflict facing couples today.

JUAN AND JEANINE SANCHEZ
High Pointe Baptist Church, Austin, Texas

D. A. & ELICIA HORTON

ENTER *the* RING

fighting together for a gospel-saturated marriage

NavPress

A NavPress resource published in alliance with Tyndale House Publishers, Inc.

NavPress is the publishing ministry of The Navigators, an international Christian organization and leader in personal spiritual development. NavPress is committed to helping people grow spiritually and enjoy lives of meaning and hope through personal and group resources that are biblically rooted, culturally relevant, and highly practical.

For more information, visit www.NavPress.com.

Enter the Ring: Fighting Together for a Gospel-Saturated Marriage

Copyright © 2017 by D. A. and Elicia Horton. All rights reserved.

A NavPress resource published in alliance with Tyndale House Publishers, Inc.

NAVPRESS and the NAVPRESS logo are registered trademarks of NavPress, The Navigators, Colorado Springs, CO. *TYNDALE* is a registered trademark of Tyndale House Publishers, Inc. Absence of ® in connection with marks of NavPress or other parties does not indicate an absence of registration of those marks.

The Team:
Don Pape, Publisher
Caitlyn Carlson, Acquisitions Editor
Helen Macdonald, Copyeditor
Jacqueline L. Nuñez, Designer

Cover photograph of boxing gloves copyright © Khakimullin Aleksandr/Shutterstock. All rights reserved. Author photograph provided by D. A. and Elicia Horton; used with permission.

Published in association with the literary agency of Wolgemuth & Associates, Inc.

Scripture quotations are taken from *The Holy Bible*, English Standard Version® (ESV®), copyright © 2001 by Crossway, a publishing ministry of Good News Publishers. Used by permission. All rights reserved. Scripture quotations marked NLT are taken from the *Holy Bible*, New Living Translation, copyright © 1996, 2004, 2015 by Tyndale House Foundation. Used by permission of Tyndale House Publishers, Inc., Carol Stream, Illinois 60188. All rights reserved.

Some of the anecdotal illustrations in this book are true to life and are included with the permission of the persons involved. All other illustrations are composites of real situations, and any resemblance to people living or dead is purely coincidental.

For information about special discounts for bulk purchases, please contact Tyndale House Publishers at csresponse@tyndale.com, or call 1-800-323-9400.

Cataloging-in-Publication Data is available.

ISBN 978-1-63146-695-3

Printed in the United States of America

23 22 21 20 19 18 17
7   6   5   4   3   2   1

To Izabelle, Lola, and Duce—
Love God with your whole being, learn from our
mistakes, and live the gospel-saturated life.

To our parents—
Thank you for going the distance for more than forty
years. You have modeled for us what it looks like
to stay together through every season of life.

Contents

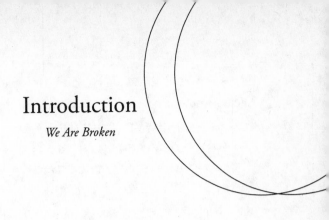

Introduction

We Are Broken

D. A.

Our wedding date was set for June 28, 2003, and we were two months away from saying "I do." But there was a problem—or, rather, many problems: Our relationship was like a roller coaster ride, and we'd been through quite a few starts, stops, ups, downs, twists, and turns (and even a malfunction or two). I was only twenty-two, and Elicia was twenty-one. We didn't have much money, we were dealing with family drama, and neither of us had ever lived on our own before. Were we too close to the wedding to call it quits? Was the only thing keeping us together the embarrassment of having another failed relationship? The pressure was mounting.

And then one Saturday evening in April, we erupted.

I was scheduled to perform a few songs at the Main Street Café in Midtown, Kansas City, but before I left my parents' house to head to the venue, Elicia and I had another heated exchange on the phone. It was probably our thousandth fight. I can't remember what it was about, but we both said things best not repeated. Needing to leave, I bluntly asked Elicia if she was coming to the event, and her reply included two sounds: a click and a dial tone.

I decided not to call her back and instead headed out.

During the last song on my set, around 10:15 p.m., Elicia walked through the door. My heart settled at the sight of her. Things were going to be okay. We would work this out, just as we had all the other times. I finished my song, shared the gospel message with the crowd, and exited stage right. As I maneuvered through the crowd, weaving in and out of small-talk conversations, I searched for Elicia. I finally saw her talking to some mutual friends. When she caught sight of me, I smiled and waved. She rolled her eyes.

Okay, so my work was cut out for me. But I felt optimistic. I pressed on until I was standing next to her, giving her a hug and whispering in her ear, "Thank you for coming, baby!" Her arms remained glued to her sides. I hated it when she did that. For me, it was the ultimate form of rejection because it reopened abandonment wounds from my childhood.

Then she told me the only reason she came was to give me back her engagement ring.

I was so stunned that I didn't quite register what was going on—until she grabbed my hand and placed the ring in it. When our eyes met again, fury rushed through me. I told her to step outside, and she said she had no time to talk because she was heading home. Then she walked past me and left the venue. I followed her outside, calling her name.

She refused to turn around. There was only one way I could stop her from getting in her car: a trigger phrase she couldn't ignore. As she reached for her keys, I told her, "I rebuke you!"

It worked. Before I could say anything else, she turned around and went off on me!

After just a few minutes, so furious I had to restrain myself from hitting her car with my fist, I walked away, down the block. Elicia followed me, taunting me every step of the way. When we started cussing each other out, we were literally standing in front of the church where I was the youth pastor!

I hit the front door of the church with my fist and took off running down the middle of the street, my signature untied Timberland boots clunking loudly with each step. When I was halfway down the block, I could hear Elicia laughing out loud.

Then I felt my cell phone buzz in my pocket. It was 12:15 a.m. Elicia's text read, "Come back here, silly boy!" I sighed with relief. It seemed as if we were both ready to talk this out.

I jogged back to the church steps, where Elicia was sitting. When I got about ten feet away from her, I opened my arms and motioned for a hug. She stood up, looked at me, and then started walking in the other direction, deeper into the neighborhood.

Now, this was not the type of neighborhood where any sane person would go for a midnight stroll. I called out for Elicia to stop, but she ignored me and kept walking. Once again I became irate and ran to catch up with her.

We met for round two directly under a streetlight at the

intersection of East Thirty-Seventh and Warwick Boulevard. The next two and a half hours were a profanity-laced shouting match. Things got bad. Really bad. Full disclosure: Drug dealers moved their business two blocks away from us because we were scaring off their clients. The people in the house on the southwest corner of the intersection were having a party, but after an hour of our fight, the partygoers turned off the music and came to the windows to watch us.

We called each other every name in the book. Elicia threatened to sue me for the cost of the wedding dress she would not be using. I told her that I was moving away from Kansas City and she would never have to worry about seeing me again.

At 4:15 a.m., my mom called. I refused to answer, so she left a voice mail telling me to come home—because, as she pointed out, nothing decent ever takes place at that hour of the morning. By this time, Elicia and I both agreed that this fight was taking us nowhere fast. We decided to give ourselves a few days to reconsider if we really wanted to get married.

By Wednesday we agreed to stay together, provided that we went through premarital counseling in the church we had been raised in. The next six weeks of counseling helped us, but it didn't heal us. That process would take years. But our brokenness didn't stop us from taking our vows to become man and wife, before God, family, and hundreds of witnesses.

*   *   *

Why did we begin this book on marriage with such an embarrassing story from our relationship? Well, first, we think there's power in being honest and transparent. And second, if God can do a great work in our relationship, no relationship is beyond His ability to repair and restore. We couldn't write a book about marriage and relationships if we weren't committed to being vulnerable about sharing the good *and* the bad. We're convinced that displaying our deficiencies allows you to see Christ's sufficiency and how He's kept us together in marriage for almost fifteen years.

No one who writes about marriage has it all together—because no one who is married has it all together! We're not here to impress you; we're here to point you to the God who works *in spite of* us, not *because of* us. Marriage is a process, and we're inviting you to look at God's work in the present tense of our lives.

Before we exchanged vows, we were two people fighting for pole position in a race to our wedding day. We had no concept of what a gospel-saturated marriage was. Our communication was poor, and our fights clearly showed that we were not on the same page. We had no idea what oneness and togetherness looked like in the face of suffering. We were both spiritually immature and used emotionalism as a crutch to stay theologically aloof. We struggled sexually—each losing respect for the other because of how much time we'd spend trying to go as far as possible without *technically* having intercourse. And financially speaking, we were on two different planets. Elicia had checking and savings accounts and good credit, and I had four bank accounts—all with red numbers!

We each had baggage, past issues, and emotional wounds that had never healed properly. Had God not intervened, we would've never made it.

If we had to summarize our marriage in one statement, it would be this: Our marriage is a union of two broken people who have both entrusted their hearts to God (through salvation in Jesus Christ) and each other while living in a broken world that keeps trying to break them apart.

As we've matured in our walk with Christ, both individually and together as husband and wife, we have seen how the world's system assaults our family daily. Marriage can be like a boxing match—and the world is our opponent (Ephesians 2:1-2). By God's grace and power (Ephesians 2:4-10), from the day we said "I do," we entered the ring as a team, and we won't stop fighting the temptations of the world until the final bell sounds!

If you're married, you and your spouse are in the middle of a fight. The world is using different tactics to distract you, trip you up, and tempt you to throw in the towel and leave the ring defeated. The world wants to destroy your marriage. But God is with you in the fight—and through forgiveness and grace He is ready to lead you, to protect you not only from the world but also from yourselves.

You have to choose to fight for your marriage. Together. No matter what you're facing.

Are you ready to enter the ring?

Our Goal

Elicia

We desire to see more gospel-saturated marriages flood the neighborhoods of our nation and world—marriages that holistically apply the gospel to every nuance of married life, becoming a vivid picture of the saving work of Jesus Christ. We want to help you fight off the assaults of the world so that your marriage can serve as one of the greatest illustrations of the gospel in our society today.

That means we're going to go through some pretty hard-hitting things, and D. A. and I are going to be honest about our own failings and struggles as we do that. You're not alone in this fight. We're going to look at what God has shown us about the institution of marriage through Scripture and how the world is assaulting his intention for it.

As believers, we have a way forward in living out an apologetic for what He's declared. But it's hard! We'll talk about the tension of two people becoming one and how, for the first few years of our marriage, we fought over which "one of us" we would become.

We're also going to get practical. We'll talk about communication, conflict, suffering, and our spiritual lives in marriage. We will work through the different roles of discipleship between husband and wife as well as the high calling of raising children—and the complications that come with it. We'll have an honest conversation about sexuality and physical intimacy as well.

And we're going to talk about money. We purposely deal with this topic because finances are often a huge struggle in marriage. We filed for bankruptcy before we'd been married five years.

In all of these areas, we do not have a squeaky-clean record! But God has taught us some things along the way, and we want to journey with you through what we've learned.

In our world today, convictions rooted in Scripture are under attack. Since marriage is a tangible illustration for the gospel, the enemy of our souls (2 Corinthians 4:4) doesn't want our marriages to thrive. We can be tempted to give up and give in when the pressures of this life squeeze us from all sides, and the world is waiting to cheer on our failure.

But through the power of the Holy Spirit (Romans 8:9-13), we can put to death those temptations, cling to our spouses, and stand with boldness against the evil forces at work. We can choose to fight *for* each other instead of *against* each other. We can choose to fight for our marriages. And with God's help, we can win.

CHAPTER I

BEAT THE WORLD TO THE PUNCH

God created man in his own image, in the image of God he created
him; male and female he created them. And God blessed them. And
God said to them, "Be fruitful and multiply and fill the earth and
subdue it, and have dominion over the fish of the sea and over the birds
of the heavens and over every living thing that moves on the earth."

GENESIS I:27-28

D. A.

The definition of marriage has been heatedly debated over
the past decade. And social media has only accelerated and
sometimes inflamed the conversation, as millions of people
contribute to the debate with witty memes, posts, and tweets
to prove their points and take shots at the opposing side.

As both sides become more polarized, and because Twitter
wars rarely lead to helpful outcomes, Elicia and I have pur-
posed to take a different approach. We want to call ourselves
and other married believers to gospel-saturated marriages.
Talking with believers across the nation about the pressing

social issues of today, we've noticed that married Christians are often distracted by the fight going on around them. They're allowing things that are temporal, not eternal, to dictate their marriages. They're choosing the world's priorities instead of God's, and the world is going to keep fighting against our marriages. We need to fight back—by choosing to live out the gospel with our spouses.

On the morning of June 26, 2015, the day the Supreme Court ruled on the definition of marriage,[1] I tweeted, "Marriage as God defines it in Scripture is a beautiful illustration of the Gospel. The Gospel shines best when in contrast to darkness." The tweet was picked up by a couple of online media outlets who were reporting on the "Christian Twitter" response to the Supreme Court decision.[2] This placed the tweet in front of people who don't usually follow me, which led to an interesting conversation between me and a person who celebrated the court ruling.

This person told me I was wrong to compare the love of two consenting adults with darkness—that I was juxtaposing God's definition of marriage. My definition of marriage, he said, is outdated and oppressive—and is evidence that Christians will lose. When I pushed back, asking exactly what we are going to lose, he warned me that Christians' opinions, ideas, and priorities regarding the definition of marriage would no longer be part of the conversation.

Politely, I asked a few follow-up questions regarding what he believed about the mission of the church, and he shared his conviction that the gospel is not objective—that any person can interpret it as he or she pleases. He told me that because the "gospel" preached by his lesbian pastor friend differed from the one I preached, the gospel itself must be subjective.

But God's Word is not subjective. It is, and will always be, the authoritative voice that each of us—me, you, the person I was in dialogue with, and the lesbian pastor—must come into submission under.

Our culture today calls for people to be accepting, affirming, and embracing of all voices, whether privileged or oppressed. However, this principle doesn't seem to hold true when a Bible-believing Christian, informed by Scripture and seeking to live a consistent biblical worldview, expresses his or her perspective. The culture of tolerance ironically cannot tolerate the biblical worldview.

Mind you, Christians don't help the situation when we resort to name-calling, sarcasm, and heartless dialogue with anyone who disagrees with us. Sadly, this carnal behavior happens not only between Christians and the unbelieving world but also among Christians who believe differently.

Fighting for a biblical definition of marriage is a challenge on many levels. But the Christian arguments for biblical marriage suffer when the world can point to the same sinfulness in Christian marriages that exists in the marriages of unbelievers. This is why we are not attacking those who agree with the Supreme Court's definition of marriage—rather, we are calling for Christians to look at their own marriages and reassess what God's Word says regarding marriage, holy living, and the Christian family.

Christians are just as susceptible as nonbelievers to issues of poor communication, frivolous spending, sexual immorality, and all other vices, because we are still wrestling with our sinful nature. This reality should humble every Christian who is married and simultaneously cause us to operate with sympathy toward those trying to navigate marriage without the indwelling of God the Holy Spirit.

As married Christians living in a pluralistic society, asking for our voices to be heard in the public sphere, we should offer to the nonbelieving world the same respect we want. When legislation directly conflicts with a biblical worldview, Christians should not only respectfully defend biblical convictions but also demonstrate those convictions in their own marriages.

Having gospel-saturated marriages allows Christians to influence the culture without compromising the convictions of the Christian faith. Our efforts can become less about engaging in a war of words on social media and more about living in marriages on mission for God's glory When we live out the implications of a gospel-saturated marriage, the biblical definition of marriage becomes clear and has greater potential to have an impact on a watching world.

Gospel-Saturated

So, what do we mean when we say "gospel saturated"? First, let's deal with the term *gospel*. When we talk about the gospel, we don't mean a generic term or genre of music—rather, the gospel includes the hope of salvation and the implication of what life looks like when a person embraces the truth of the gospel. This is how the Bible lays out the gospel message:

- Every human being is born dead in sin (Psalm 51:5; Ephesians 2:1-3), enslaved to sin (John 8:34), and completely unable to save him- or herself from the rightful wrath of God (Romans 2:5-6).

- God sent Jesus—God fully incarnated in human flesh (John 1:1-14)—to die in our place (Mark 10:45). He lived the perfect life no sinful human can live (Hebrews 7:26). He was buried only to rise from the grave, showing that His payment of shed blood (Ephesians 1:7) was approved by God (Romans 4:24-25).

- Sinners—from every ethnicity, gender, and socioeconomic situation—who hear the gospel, believe it, and confess with their mouth that Jesus is Lord and that God raised Him from the dead (Romans 1:16; 10:9-17) will be saved from enduring God's wrath (Romans 5:9). And they will receive eternal life (John 17:3) by grace through faith and enjoy a rightly reconciled relationship with God because of Christ's finished work (2 Corinthians 5:17-21).

Second, let's talk about the term *saturated*. Something is saturated when it has completely absorbed something else. Once, when I was preparing for a trip out of town, I packed a small bottle of liquid starch to use when ironing my clothes. During my flight, the top of the bottle came off. When I opened the suitcase, I saw that my clothes were completely saturated with starch. While saturated clothes are certainly not ideal, a marriage completely saturated by the gospel message is a beautiful thing. A gospel-saturated marriage is one in which the husband and wife strive to apply the gospel's content and implications in every area of their marriage.

Let's move from the theoretical to the practical by using Colossians 1:3-8 as a case study on *how* to live out gospel saturation.

> We always thank God, the Father of our Lord Jesus Christ, when we pray for you, since we heard of your faith in Christ Jesus and of the love that you have for all the saints, because of the hope laid up for you in heaven. Of this you have heard before in the word of the truth, the gospel, which has come to you, as indeed in the whole world it is bearing fruit and increasing—as it also does among you, since the day you heard it and understood the grace of God in truth, just as you learned it from Epaphras our beloved fellow servant. He is a faithful minister of Christ on your behalf and has made known to us your love in the Spirit.

This passage captures what a gospel-saturated life looks like. Imagine the impact a marriage can have when it comprises two believers indwelled by the Holy Spirit and living this kind of gospel-saturated life! According to the book of Colossians, a gospel-saturated life consists of three things: (1) a regular practice of thankfulness and prayer; (2) a personification of faith, love, and hope; and (3) a healthy commitment to the local church.

A Regular Practice of Thankfulness and Prayer

Paul begins his letter to the Christians in Colossae by informing them that he and Timothy pray for them consistently—and that their prayers include thankfulness to God for these Christians.

The phrasing Paul uses in the Greek tells us that his prayers for these Christians were daily. One lexicon defines the word *pray* as "to petition deity."[3] Paul is daily seeking the face of the sovereign God of the universe—and praying not for himself but for the saints in Colossae.

Can you say the same regarding your prayer life and the spouse you live with? Do you spend regular amounts of time praying both with and for your spouse?

Elicia

Early in our marriage, D. A. and I didn't make times of prayer a priority. When moments of crisis hit, we approached God's throne of grace together—but sadly, when the crisis subsided, we were not disciplined to continue the practice. We had no problem praying for each other during our personal time with God; however, prayer together was limited to mealtime and bedtime. When you and another person have entered into a covenant, share a bed, and are both indwelled by the Holy Spirit, not praying together is unhealthy.

It wasn't until we were five years into our marriage that we began praying together regularly. Sadly, it took situations such as entering the pastorate, filing for bankruptcy, making job transitions, and having fallouts with family and friends to drive us to pray together. These times of prayer ranged between five minutes and more than an hour. We began to notice that when we poured our hearts out together before God and laced our prayers with thanksgiving, He answered us quickly. Not every answer was a yes, so we began to ask God to prepare our hearts to receive His will.

The togetherness we gained through consistent times of prayer—which, again, we want to stress were sometimes as short as five minutes—benefited our relationship in many ways. As we made ourselves vulnerable and expressed our anxieties and fears, "my" struggle turned into "our" struggle. And when we took our struggles to God, we knew He was with us in whatever we faced! As we walked in vulnerability together, we experienced a renewed desire to protect each other's hearts, not only from the enemy of our souls and the world but also from each other.

Pride is the great assassin of marriages. And prayer is the ultimate antidote for pride. Coming together in prayer creates the humility to confess wrongs and extend forgiveness. Words of affirmation and thanksgiving become a regular rhythm in the relationship. Togetherness in prayer is a key aspect of a gospel-saturated marriage.

A Personification of Faith, Love, and Hope

D. A.

In Colossians 1:4-6, Paul highlights the evidence that the saints in Colossae were living out the gospel: their *faith* in Christ, the *love* they had for all the saints, and their *hope* in heaven. Simply put, their lifestyle was in harmony with the gospel. Their lives showed that Christ the risen Lord reigned in their hearts.

The quality of someone's faith is measured by the quality of the object in which that person places his or her faith. Take a chair, for example. My faith in a chair can only be as strong as the chair. If it is a weak chair, then I have weak faith that the chair will hold me. If it is a strong chair, then I have strong faith. The evidence of my faith becomes visible when I decide to sit in the chair. The phrase "faith in Christ" in Colossians 1:4 shows that the believers found security of salvation in Jesus, not in themselves.

As Christians, we are often tempted to put our faith in things other than Jesus Christ. Our entire lives before we were saved consisted of a cyclical trial-and-error process of placing our faith in temporal things that never ultimately protected our hearts. The world regularly throws various temptations toward us that can cause us to seek to put our marriages in the hands of something outside of Christ. Sadly, sometimes marriage itself becomes an idol, and spouses wrap up their identity in their relationship with each other. Or perhaps a dream home becomes the security blanket in a marriage. Maybe for some people, their spouse's job—or their own—forms their identity, and they feel that as long as they're collecting a salary with benefits, they're secure. Yet when the trials of life come and the idols of their heart are exposed—when they're laid off, lose their home, face profound conflict with their spouse—their once-solid marriage is now skating on thin, cracking ice. Their faith was weak because they placed it in temporary things. Gospel saturation calls us to place our faith in Someone who never changes.

Hebrews 11:1 says, "Faith is the assurance of things hoped for, the conviction of things not seen." Faith for the Christian is anchored not in some*thing* but in some*one*—the God-man, Jesus Christ. He alone has been tried, tested, and found absolutely true. He is the one who will never leave us or forsake us (Hebrews 13:5). It is impossible to live out the implications of a gospel-saturated life if our faith is not rooted in Jesus Christ.

One evidence of our faith in Christ is a genuine love for other Christians. You can't have a gospel-saturated marriage and you can't truly and wholly love your spouse if Jesus Christ alone is not the object of your faith. This is not a mere verbal profession of Jesus being Lord—rather, it is *living* as if He is Lord, striving to obey His commands from Scripture. When you do this, your love for Christ, for your spouse, for all other saints, and for the entire nonbelieving world becomes evident through your "good works" toward others (Titus 3:8, 14). Your good works must first take place in your home, toward those who live with you, and then these good works produce a natural outflow of love, placing your marriage on display for the glory of Christ.

Displaying this kind of love and marriage takes time and discipline. It takes a forgiving heart dedicated to building a godly future with the person you have entered into a covenant with. The love you express toward your spouse should resemble what we read in Romans 5:8—that while we were in our lowest spiritual state before salvation (dead in sin, slaves to sin, and separated from God), God demonstrated His love for us by punishing His Son on the cross in our place. If God loved us at our lowest, then no one has the excuse to not do the same for his or her spouse. No matter how our spouses sin, or if they show arrogant stubbornness in an argument or reluctance to engage fully in the spiritual journey alongside us, we should never stop showing unfailing love.

This type of love is possible, and we know this because Paul acknowledged that the saints in Colossae were practicing it. Their motivation to love this way was a result of their hope in heaven—they had heard the Word of Truth, the gospel. Since marriage is an illustration for the gospel, as Paul says in Ephesians 5:25-32, we must assess what love looks like in a gospel-saturated marriage. Paul says Christ demonstrates His love for the church by giving Himself up for her, to have the privilege of sanctifying her and cleansing her with the Word of God. The outcome Christ is aiming for is a purified and spotless bride.

A gospel-saturated marriage recognizes the hope that carries our hearts through every storm: Holiness in heaven is the secured eternal reality for those of us who are saved and who are part of the bride of Christ. This hope, which is guaranteed (Ephesians 1:13-14), should drive us to emulate the love of Christ toward our spouses by dying to self, holding each other accountable, and regularly digesting God's Word together. Doing this over the course of time will produce in us a level of spiritual maturity that allows us to not be blown over by every wind of false teaching, temptation, and emotion.

A Healthy Commitment to the Local Church

Spiritual maturity, as described in Ephesians 4:14-16, is not designed to be lived out in isolation. Spiritual maturity is affirmed and made evident when we're living in community together. Our marriages will bloom and blossom alongside other marriages when we're planting and rooting ourselves together in local churches. This is why gospel-saturated marriages have strong commitments to the local church.

Colossians 1:5-8 highlights the commitment of the saints in Colossae to the local church. Epaphras was the vessel the Lord used to expose the saints in Colossae to the gospel. Paul calls him a "fellow servant," faithful to Christ. This description clues us in that Epaphras was dependable and reliable (faithful) and selflessly met the needs of the people in the church (a servant).

This type of availability fostered community. Meeting the needs of others naturally produces togetherness. When we live out this reality as couples by seeking to holistically meet the needs of our spouses, we will then have a posture and sensitivity to meet the emotional, physical, and spiritual needs of those in our local church.

More than fifty times in the New Testament we see the phrase "one another." Most of the occurrences deal with the interpersonal relationships of those in the body of Christ. Imagine the impact our local churches can have on broken communities when numerous gospel-saturated marriages engage both inside and outside the walls of the church.

But make no mistake: Operating at this level of togetherness takes sacrifice. We have to choose to carve out time for relationships among the saints, regardless of their marital status. As we devote ourselves to one another (Romans 12:10), over the course of time we will honor those in our local church above ourselves. Doing this produces harmony (12:16) that motivates us to not pass judgment on one another (14:13). During times of community building, we begin to take down the filters we use in public. All our bad habits, emotional scars, personality traits, and quirks begin to come out. It's important for us to welcome and embrace the nonfiltered, authentic, broken, and spiritually developing brothers and sisters in the faith. This is what it looks like to accept one another as Christ accepted us (15:7).

When this type of life becomes the rhythm of our marriages and homes, our times of celebration and worship in the church will feel like family reunions! We'll have equal concern for one another (1 Corinthians 12:25), strive to serve one another (Galatians 5:13), fight against devouring one another (5:15), and be prone to carrying one another's burdens (6:2). These actions will produce fruits of tenderheartedness, forgiveness, and truthfulness toward one another (Ephesians 4:32; Colossians 3:9, 13). During times of suffering, we will naturally be driven to encourage one another (1 Thessalonians 4:18; Hebrews 13:3), build one another up (1 Thessalonians 5:11) instead of grumbling at one another (James 5:9), and simply love one another (1 John 3:11, 23, 4:7-2; 2 John 5).

Imagine if all these attributes are first present in our marriages. Then think of the marriages in our local churches making these things tangible. The darkness of the world will be pushed back as we strive to maintain the rhythm of gospel-saturated lives. The world will take notice.

The Three Cs
Now that we've established what a gospel-saturated life looks like, let's look a little closer at marriage itself. As we wrote earlier, our marriage is a union of two broken people who have both entrusted their hearts to God (through salvation in Jesus Christ) and each other while living in a broken world that keeps trying to break them apart.

We believe the greatest potential for living out a gospel-saturated marriage is when each spouse has embraced Christ as Lord and Savior. However, we recognize not every Christian is married to another Christian. If this is your reality, don't lose heart. You can live out a gospel-saturated life in such a way that the Lord uses it to bring your nonbelieving spouse to salvation. Your faithfulness—and your reliance on God's grace in loving your spouse—will act as an example in your local church.

To understand marriage further, we have to answer a common question: When does God consider a couple married? Couples often ask us this question, and we must discern why the person or couple wants our perspective. Sometimes a couple is living in a cohabitating relationship and declares they are in love and do not need a piece of paper to tell them that. Other times, people express their desire to have a commitment ceremony rather than a traditional marriage ceremony—so they can make an initial commitment but with the option not to maintain it long term. We believe neither of these choices reflect marriage as defined by God.

We view marriage primarily as an institution created and ordained by God to serve as a tangible illustration of the gospel message and its implications. Inside the framework of marriage, especially among believers, we should find self-sacrificing love, patience, loyalty, and endurance. It is possible for nonbelievers, who are image bearers of God, to enjoy long-lasting marriages possessing these same characteristics. However, for Christians, marriage does not exist merely for the purpose of enjoying life; rather, our lives should be so saturated with the gospel that people will want to know how and why we're making our marriage *work*—giving us the opportunity to point them toward Christ as Savior.

Working in cooperation with the Holy Spirit, Christians who are married—and encountering the same struggles all marriages face—can unveil what it looks like to find victory over the assaults of the world. The conviction to endure the fight must root back to an understanding that marriage is God's idea. None of us can truly endure the fight without Him.

God's desire for marriage to thrive is amazing to see. The concept is on display in both the opening and closing of the Bible, His love letter to His covenant people.[4] And the entire human race traces its lineage back to the first marriage—Adam and Eve's. In Acts 17:26 Paul says Adam was the man God used to bring forth all the ethnicities of the world, and in Genesis 3:20 Adam named his wife Eve because she was the mother of all living human beings. In Genesis 3 the fall of man introduced sin and death universally to the human race (Romans 5:12-21), and this fall provides us with the backdrop to the second and best marriage of all, found in the last parts of Scripture. This is the marriage between the second Adam—Jesus Christ—and His bride: the people of God, all of redeemed humanity.

God's heart and design for marriage is why we must look to Scripture to discern when He considers a couple married. The Bible does not specifically declare a point at which God accepts a couple as married. The answer is more nuanced. Dr. Andreas Kostenberger provides a helpful definition: "Marriage is a

covenant, a sacred bond between a man and a woman insti-
tuted by and publicly entered into before God and normally
consummated by sexual intercourse."[5] Similarly, our understanding of marriage is rooted in three biblical principles:
(1) cultural declaration, (2) ceremony, and (3) consummation.

Cultural Declaration

Throughout human history, couples have needed to cross
various cultural hurdles before society would recognize their
marriage. In the Hammurabi Empire, "the largest category of
laws . . . focused on marriage and the family. Parents arranged
marriages for their children. After marriage, the parties
involved signed a marriage contract; without it, no one was
considered legally married."[6] In precolonized Aztecan culture
in Mexico, "marriage rarely took place without the consent
of the parents, with the marriage partner usually chosen by
them."[7] In ancient Rome a legal marriage was necessary to
have legitimate children. A marriage would be considered
legal when a man and a woman fulfilled the requirements of
conubium, which mandated that "spouses were Roman citizens, were of sufficient age or physical maturity, and lacked
a close blood relationship."[8]

In the United States, each state has different regulations
for couples who wish to be recognized as married. Elicia and
I were married in the state of Missouri and were mandated
by law to apply for and purchase a marriage license. In addition, after the ceremony took place, the officiating clergy
member and two witnesses of legal age were required to sign

the license. (When I was twelve, I had the privilege of serving as best man in my older brother's wedding. However, because I was not of legal age in the state of Missouri, I was not allowed to sign the marriage license.) Finally, for a marriage in Missouri to be considered legal, the document had to be signed, sealed, mailed, and then received by the county clerk within fourteen days of the ceremony.

In Romans 13:1-7 and 1 Peter 2:17, Christians are called to live under submission to the authorities in their society. Therefore, in support of this, believers who desire to be married should go through the proper channels to receive recognition from governing authorities. However, because civilizations have had different customs and we live in a country where federal law now allows couples of the same sex to be married, it's important to note that cultural declaration is only one of three nuances necessary for a marriage to be recognized in the eyes of God.

Ceremony

A ceremony of some sort should take place in addition to the cultural declaration. Prior to receiving Christianity, indigenous Mexican couples whose parents blessed their desire to be married would present themselves before an Aztec priest. The priest would take their hands and begin asking a series of questions that concluded with confirming the personal desire of each person to be married. Then the priest would tie part of the woman's veil to the man's garment and lead the two around a kindled fire seven times at the bride's house.[9]

In Jewish culture, the journey to marriage has two parts: a time of engagement and the marriage itself. Historically the former would last for about a year, while the latter would be for a lifetime. The public wedding ceremony connected these two parts.[10] For modern marriages, the ceremony acts as the framework for the covenant both parties are entering into before God, each other, and all present witnesses.

Arguably the first ceremony in Scripture can be found in Genesis 2:18-23. Since there is no specific biblical framework for a wedding ceremony, we can best define it, based on this passage, as a man and woman joyfully coming together before God to express their desire to remain exclusively together from that moment on. However, the covenantal language between God and the newly wedded couple is found in Genesis 1:26-31, which parallels Genesis 2:15-25. God states He created both man and woman in His image, giving distinction between the human race and all other forms of creation. God mandated for Adam and Eve to populate the earth with other humans, thus showing the biological necessity for both to participate in procreation. God then delegated humans to steward creation while having dominion over it. The task is too heavy for one person to carry alone, thus the need for both the man and woman—and in the future all their offspring—to work in harmony to carry out the task.

Genesis 2:8-17 provides us with clarity about God's covenantal instructions to Adam. Prior to the creation of Eve, God gave Adam a job: stewarding the Garden of Eden. Adam was to obey God perfectly in two ways: tending the Garden and not eating fruit from the tree of the knowledge of good and evil. Disobedience would break the covenant, and death would be the result.

Genesis 2:18 is the first record in Scripture of God saying something is "not good." This passage contrasts the creation story. All things God created in Genesis 1–2 were good because God the creator is infinitely good. In verse 18 God recognizes that it is not good for man to be alone, and He then makes a complementary helper for Adam.

The word *helper* means, as you might expect, a person who helps someone else—and not as a slave or servant, but rather as one who is supportive of the task at hand. In the context of this passage, the helper—or better yet, supporter—was necessary for Adam to fulfill the task God required. Old Testament scholar Bruce Waltke says, "The word *helper*, used for God sixteen of the nineteen times it appears in the Old Testament, signifies the woman's essential contribution, not inadequacy."[11] God saying that he would make Adam "a helper fit for him" (verse 18) means that she, too, would be an image bearer of God. This distinguishes her from every other form of creation, thus showing God's design for humanity. The mission to steward creation would be shared by a man and a woman who desired to walk in obedience to God.

Verses 21-22 of Genesis 2 say, "The LORD God caused a deep sleep to fall upon the man, and while he slept took one of his ribs and closed up its place with flesh. And the rib that the LORD God had taken from the man he made into a woman and brought her to the man." It has been said God did not select a bone from Adam's head so that the woman would rule over man or become proud, nor from his feet that he would walk all over her; rather, He brought her forth from Adam's rib to create an environment of equality, protection, and modesty (by the husband serving as her covering).[12] Adam receives Eve with great joy and verbally declares the connectedness they will share and their desire to remain exclusively together from that moment on.

Consummation

The act of consummation is necessary for a marriage to be recognized by God. Genesis 2:24-25 says, "A man shall leave his father and his mother and hold fast to his wife, and they shall become one flesh. And the man and his wife were both naked and were not ashamed." These two verses are commentary by the author Moses, intended to help readers understand God's purpose for marriage. Jesus affirms God's intentions in Matthew 19:5: "A man shall leave his father and his mother and hold fast to his wife, and the two shall become one flesh." The apostle Paul also quotes this passage in Ephesians 5:31, emphasizing how marriage between a man and a woman is an illustration of Christ's love for His bride, the church.

One definition of the word *consummation* is "the time at which something is finally completed,"[13] and obviously the act of sexual intercourse places the final piece of the framework for a recognized marriage in the eyes of God. However, Genesis 2:24-25 points to a oneness in marriage that should exist beyond that of sexual intimacy between the husband and wife. The language of the two becoming one flesh speaks also to the intimate unity between the husband and wife to the exclusion of all others.[14]

We see a further picture of this oneness between the couple through the description of them as "naked and . . . not ashamed." At the beginning of human history there were no fears of abuse, exploitation, infidelity, manipulation, or sexual deviancy because sin had not yet entered the picture. The nakedness of Adam and Eve unveils the fact that each of them had no fear of being exposed. They were walking in complete obedience to God and were at the center of His will.

God had designed Adam and Eve for togetherness in matrimony and mission, and He blessed their union. Moses communicated the necessity of oneness because the readers of Genesis were living in a world tainted by sin, broken family structures, and a loss of the original nakedness (Genesis 3:1-7). In addition, marriage ceremonies after the first one in Genesis 2 would involve parents or guardians of both the bride and groom, necessitating a recognition of possible family tensions that would surround the newlyweds after the ceremony and consummation took place.

Moses introduces what we call the leave-and-cleave principle, where both the husband and wife place each other as the priority over all other preexisting relationships. The newlyweds continue to love their premarriage family structures; however, the new marriage takes precedence.

The Hebrew word for *cleave* means "be united, joined, i.e., be in a close association"[15]—in other words, being in continued togetherness. This implies a long-lasting togetherness that grows deeper over the course of marriage. The necessity for oneness and togetherness in marriage is a theme throughout Scripture.

Be a Billboard

Now that you have a solid foundation for defining marriage according to God's standards, you can beat the world to the punch. The greatest apologetic for marriage as God intended is a gospel-saturated marriage in which both the husband and wife believe the content of the gospel, place their trust in Christ to save them by grace through faith, and work to apply the gospel in every area of their lives.

Our world needs to see every Christian couple fighting together as one through the storms of life. The gospel compels us to do this. As gospel-saturated husbands and wives, we express thankfulness toward each other, pray together regularly, ensure our faith is placed rightly in Christ, love each other as God loves us, and embrace biblical hope together—all while living in community with the saints in our local churches. When we do this, the world will watch us draw closer to each other—and God—each passing day.

To our brothers and sisters married to nonbelieving spouses: You can offer a solid gospel witness through expressing thankfulness to your spouses, asking them to pray with you regularly, and inviting them to engage in mutual friendships with other believers inside and outside your local church. As you sow seeds of a healthy gospel witness, we pray that the Lord will send other believers to water those seeds—and that ultimately God will draw your spouses to salvation (1 Corinthians 3:5-9).

The battle for the togetherness Scripture prescribes does not come automatically with a cultural declaration, a ceremony, and consummation. It takes each spouse committing to walk in step with the Holy Spirit who indwells them—and when they grieve (Ephesians 4:30) and quench His work (1 Thessalonians 5:19), they should humble themselves by confessing and repenting. A gospel-saturated marriage is not perfect—in fact, it's messy because the Holy Spirit is progressively sanctifying both spouses. The world needs to see the beautiful struggle of Christian marriages, the tension of two striving for oneness. As we do this, our marriages will serve as a billboard for the gospel message. When we dedicate ourselves to living out gospel-saturated marriages, we're beating the world to the punch, no longer contributing to the lie that God's definition of marriage doesn't work. Instead, we get to proclaim the gospel through marriage, sharing the Good News with people from every nation, tribe, and tongue.

CHAPTER 2

WHICH "ONE"?

*He answered, "Have you not read that he who created them from the
beginning made them male and female, and said, 'Therefore a man
shall leave his father and his mother and hold fast to his wife, and the
two shall become one flesh'? So they are no longer two but one flesh.
What therefore God has joined together, let not man separate."*

MATTHEW 19:4-6

D. A.

Marriage is a beautiful struggle of two becoming one. And
the struggle is best summed up by this question: Which *one*
of the spouses will the two become? Spouses constantly face
tension over preferences, rhythms of life, and personalities.
We may clash over whose family to visit on holidays, where
to eat for dinner, and how to spend money. And in these
moments, the marriage begins to resemble whomever is
more dominant, while the spouse who is passive or passive-
aggressive takes a backseat.

But a gospel-saturated marriage strives for oneness—not
a oneness that defaults to one spouse or the other, but a

oneness that reflects the new creation of the marriage. The clearest picture of oneness we have is our relationship with God through the finished work of Christ: We were born dead in sin (Ephesians 2:1-3) and separated from Him, yet Jesus ransomed us from out of our sin slavery (Mark 10:45), purchased us with His blood (Ephesians 1:7), and made us new creations in Him (2 Corinthians 5:17). The gospel simply announces a reconciled relationship between a perfectly holy God and those who were once separated from Him because of their sin. Because of Christ, we are separated no longer; rather we are one with Him.

We see this oneness of relationship mirrored in Adam and Eve in the Garden of Eden before the Fall (Genesis 1–3). Ever since they chose sin, spouses have been tempted to remain holistically separate: conversationally, emotionally, financially, and sexually. But therein lies the beauty of a gospel-saturated marriage: It takes the gospel oneness that both spouses have with God and infuses it into each and every area of temptation to live separately in marriage.

We will take time to work through each of these areas in the coming chapters. But in this chapter, we want to work through what lies at the root of the struggle with oneness that couples face, because only in understanding that—and how to heal from that—can spouses move toward wholeness in every part of their relationship. And the main thing that keeps married couples from healthy and holistic relationships is relational brokenness. For Elicia and me, emotional brokenness has produced tension in our relationship for almost thirty years. Notice we said "relationship," not "mar-riage." Because we met each other when we were kids, our emotional baggage goes back three decades.

Elicia and I met in the summer of 1989 when our respective parents decided to help with our local church's children's evangelism ministry. On Saturdays, our church would go into more than a dozen housing projects to put on church services for the children who lived there.

Because our families are both Latino and speak and understand Spanish, we were paired one Saturday to minister in the Mexican American community on the west side of Kansas City. After we had finished the day of evangelism with our parents, Elicia's family invited my mother and me over to their house. Elicia, her older brother, and I enjoyed the afternoon together. Our friendship grew in the months that followed.

One Saturday night the next summer, I received a call from my cousin. The girl he liked was on the other line. She had told him she would not become his girlfriend unless I became the boyfriend of her best friend—Elicia. Now, by this time I had a crush on Elicia, but I'd kept my feelings to myself. I was scared that if I told her I liked her, she wouldn't like me back. I didn't think I could deal with that level of rejection—if she rejected me, I didn't know how we would remain friends. And, more practically, my mom told me I couldn't have a girlfriend—or even receive phone calls from girls. Even if Elicia did say yes, I didn't know how I could hide our relationship from my mom since our families went to church and did ministry together.

But I still agreed to ask Elicia to be my girlfriend. The girl my cousin liked agreed to be his girlfriend and then put Elicia on the phone. (I feel as though today's teenagers have it so easy: All of this could've been taken care of over text messages rather than an awkward three-way telephone call.) After a few minutes of small talk, Elicia agreed to be my girlfriend.

Immediately after I hung up, I felt anxious. When my mom asked me why I had been on the phone, I told her I was talking to my cousin. She didn't probe any further, and I felt as if I were home-free.

The next day at church, my family went to the first service and Elicia's family attended the second, so we did not cross paths. But that evening, everything came undone.

I walked into the church for the evening service and saw my cousin, his brother, Elicia, her friend, and a few other friends all sitting in the back row of the sanctuary. Our church was one of the first megachurches in Kansas City, seating around fifteen hundred people. Our sanctuary also functioned as a basketball gym and restaurant, so you can envision the magnitude of the place.

After we had sung the last song before the sermon, we all sat down in that back pew of the huge church. Elicia was at one end of the row, I was at the other end, and all our friends and family were between us. As soon as the pastor started preaching, Elicia asked everybody to pass down a friendship ring and tell me it was from her.

Now, I have to set the context for what happened next. My mom had shaped my worldview in many ways, especially when it came to relationships, and she had always told me that to a girl, a ring of any kind means marriage—so you can imagine that my understanding of what was happening was very different. When my cousin handed me the ring, all I could think about was how I was going to have to explain to my mom that I was getting married. I came to church hoping to avoid a blowup, and now I was being confronted with making a lifelong commitment before entering fifth grade! So at that moment I stood up and yelled out, "I can't do this anymore!" Then I threw the ring on the ground and ran out of the church.

Elicia

That moment shattered my young heart. Over the course of our relationship, when tensions have escalated between D. A. and me, I've often blacked out, unable to remember what I said or did. But my first trip to heartbreak city? Let's just say I remember everything vividly.

Here I was, the confused tomboy who outran boys at recess and saw arm wrestling as a sport, putting my heart on the line to show this fool how much I really liked him. I had spent my milk money on that neon-colored friendship ring. When D. A. threw it on the ground and ran out of the church, he hit a major artery. I went home and told my sister how he'd broken my heart. (Many years later, after the announcement of our engagement, my sister asked me seriously whether I was secure in D. A.'s love for me—she remembered how deeply he had hurt me when we were younger.) What he did to me that day was so hurtful and embarrassing that, in all honesty, it took me years to forgive him.

From that young age, I began to build a wall of self-preservation to protect my heart from being hurt by him again. We had a lot of mutual friends and went to the same church, so we found ourselves hanging in the same circles.

But even in this time of rebuilding, our friendship was confusing. Our conversations tended toward one of two extremes. Either D. A. would joke around so much I could never tell whether he was serious or playing, or he would try to play matchmaker and hook me up with one of his friends from his neighborhood. I really struggled with how he perceived me—I wondered if he thought I was promiscuous. I would always walk away disheartened.

Already, starting all the way back in fifth grade, we were building barriers to our future oneness.

Barriers to Oneness
For D. A. and me, that day in church foreshadowed what much of our early relationship would be like. We were both so immature in more ways than one, and we would inflict much more hurt on each other. Since we had never talked through my hurt from that moment in church, both of us became passive-aggressive. For the next ten years, we threw verbal blows and jabs at each other, sprinkling humor into our interactions only to save face.

We approached our twenties feeling emotionally drained from relational drama. Eventually, we tried to reconnect as friends—and that led to conversations two or three hours at a time on the phone. Sharing a level of mutual vulnerability not only allowed us to set our hurt aside and connect but also provided space for us to begin investing emotionally in each other. Shortly after, we began to consider each other as prospects, not just for dating but also for marriage. Casual dating frustrated us. We both wanted something permanent. But even as we desired to move toward marriage, we didn't recognize the significant ways in which we would struggle to become one.

When people hear our story, they often ask if we were ready to get married. In short, no, we weren't. But we both believe that marriage forges a certain level of maturity, even for those who "aren't ready." Gaining that maturity requires recognizing the barriers to oneness that lie in your path. Woundedness happens in every relationship, bit by bit, piece by piece. The brokenness we bring to our relationships creates further barriers to oneness as we move forward. These specific barriers may look different for different people, but for those who are seeking a gospel-saturated marriage, spiritual immaturity and family relationships are two common ones. And only in identifying our specific brokenness can we take the first steps toward healing.

Spiritual Immaturity

When I was younger, my view of salvation played a significant role in how I viewed relationships in general. In my early walk with Christ, I was taught to regard salvation as works based—that my words, actions, attitudes, or lack thereof would determine whether I was truly saved. I didn't fully comprehend the depth or certainty of God's love for me and the implications of true salvation by faith through grace alone. And because I was ignorant of this beautiful truth for so many years, my concept of love in general was as unstable as my life was.

I am embarrassed to say that I hopped in and out of several relationships. Whenever things went sour and I wasn't feeling that person anymore, I walked away. I rarely put up a fight. If I did, it was out of mere retaliation. Whenever I was over-whelmed by outside pressures, I allowed the enemy, my flesh, and the world to influence me to believe I wasn't truly saved or captured by God's grace. This meant I would put absolutely no effort into walking upright. I was extremely carnal, emotion-ally and spiritually bent out of shape. My guard was down. As the book of Ephesians describes, I was, as those who lacked faith, "tossed to and fro by the waves" of uncertainty (4:14).

D. A. and I fought so much before we were married—like cats and dogs is an understatement. Let's just say if we had our own reality TV show back then, our ratings would be chart topping. Our lives were drama filled and unpredict-able: One minute we'd be passionately worshiping the Lord at church, and the next we'd be breaking up in a Denny's parking lot late at night.

Because our spiritual journeys had a lot of similarities, we were truly like the blind leading the blind. We valued dating more than discipleship. We allowed our flesh to govern us more so than the Holy Spirit. We put more effort into practicing our kissing techniques than our spiritual disciplines. We studied each other more than we studied God's Word, and we would eloquently draft the most creative love letters to each other while never consistently cracking open God's love letter to us.

I did not fully understand the unconditional love of God and always felt the need to work for it. Consequently, I didn't understand the genuine love D. A. had for me and felt the need to work for it too. I didn't realize that unconditional love meant no strings attached. No prerequisites. No hoops to jump through. No extra credit points needed.

Our Savior expressed ultimate love for us when He willingly endured all our sin and shame on the cross. He loves us that much. We don't have to work for it. In our own merit, we can't earn it. Even when we still sin, oh how He loves us! As you and your spouse develop a deeper understanding of, and appreciation for, God's love, you both will desire to mature in your love for God in return, which will then mature your love for each other.

We gain spiritual maturity when we have a healthy understanding of the gospel, salvation, and the love of God. But having an unhealthy understanding of these foundational truths renders us immature. If we want gospel-saturated marriages, we need to seek to demolish this barrier to oneness.

Family Relationships

D. A.

Family structures play such a significant role in how each of us grows and develops. Every family has its own unique complexities, values, and beliefs. And while family structures don't create uniformity, they do create a culture—similarities that family members tend to adopt.

I've encountered only a small number of people who pay attention to the impact of family structures when they first consider a relationship. On the other hand, I've known many people who become very concerned with family structures once they've crossed into marriage. What does this tell us? The families we came from do in fact play a major role in marriage—and the structures we grew up with can be a barrier to oneness in marriage. Taking two completely different family structures and joining them together to form a new family unit doesn't make all the former challenges disappear. Rather, these challenges are often highlighted, like a mustard stain on the backdrop of a clean white T-shirt.

No matter how healthy your or your spouse's family is, you both bring different expectations and experiences to marriage. Elicia's and my family were polar opposites, which added another layer of complexity to our emotional brokenness.

Elicia came from a codependent family rhythm. She was used to doing life in community with her family, but they had unhealthy expectations and an emotional reliance on everyone participating in functions and gatherings—mandating togetherness but rarely celebrating it freely. They gathered for each person's birthday and every major holiday and would not bless the food until everybody was present. If a family member was absent on more than a few occasions within a short period of time, tension and conflict were bound to erupt.

My family, on the other hand, was very independent. Each person normally functioned on his or her own, and togetherness was not a priority. My oldest brother, Darren, lived with his biological mom (my dad's ex-wife) in Oklahoma. He was thirteen years older than me and, sadly, passed away when I was ten. My other brother, Raymond, who is seven years older than I am, left the house when I was twelve. During most of my coming-of-age years, I felt more like an only child rather than the baby in a family of three boys. My dad worked the third shift most of my life, and we were used to him not being around on holidays and birthdays. My mother and I would go out to eat, go to the movies, and even spend Thanksgiving alone before going to another family member's house. On a typical evening, my mom would be eating dinner by herself in one room while my dad would be in the bedroom watching TV, and I would be alone in another room. We came together when it was necessary, but we were used to doing things alone.

In our first few years of marriage, our two different philosophies clashed regularly. Initially, all the regular invites over to Elicia's parents' house for birthday and holiday celebrations didn't bother me. However, over the course of time, when the stress of absent or tardy family members became a hot topic of conversation, I began to see things turn toxic. And when we had children, I wanted to develop our own family traditions instead of deferring to invitations from my in-laws.

People often celebrate similarities while devaluing differences. We would rather share stories of similar upbringings and commonalities than talk about each other's broken pasts and differences. Think about the famous dating games back in the day. The goal was to find a dating prospect who answered with similar opinions, likes, and interests. You rarely heard someone choose the person with completely different views! Differences can very easily turn into conflict, and differences in family backgrounds can be a source of struggle in marriage. If not dealt with through healthy communication and a willingness to stand together as one, families of origin can—often unwittingly—undermine the husband and wife's relationship. However, all barriers can be turned into opportunities for oneness—if the couple works together to grow and love each other in the hard situations.

In our case, Elicia and I had to spend time in a heart-to-heart conversation in order to come to a mutual understanding: We needed to not bring the rhythm from either one of our families of origin into our marriage but rather develop our own interdependent family rhythm. The gospel provided us with clarity on how to develop this interdependency, which was necessary for the two of us to become a *new* "one."

Becoming One

Elicia

Oneness doesn't happen all at once. It takes hard work. It takes dependence on God. It takes intentionality and awareness of where growth needs to happen. As D. A. and I pursued one-ness, we had to develop practices that connected to gospel convictions. (We'll unpack these more specifically in the next several chapters.) By God's grace, we who were once living in tension as we strived to define our marriage identity are now progressing toward oneness, mutually desiring greater togetherness. We are still in process, but we are encouraged by what God has already done.

One of the greatest compliments about our growth came from a pastor whom D. A. served alongside in Kansas City. Pastor Bob Clayton was counted among the older pastors on our elder board—and arguably the most seasoned one. He and his wife, Pat, would regularly approach us to share their assessments of our interactions with each other and the members of our congregation. We were surprised one of the first times this happened because we didn't know they were watching us so closely. They mentioned that for a few months they had been watching my countenance every time D. A. would share a personal story or powerful points from the Scriptures during a sermon. They said they were deeply encouraged as they watched me follow along with every word, like every other member in the congregation, as the Lord was communicating through D. A.

Bob and Pat indicated that often the integrity of a pastor's communication can be measured by the look on his wife's face. If she appears disgruntled or even disinterested, it's possible that either she cannot deal with her husband's hypocrisy or something else is wrong in the home. Bob and

Pat affirmed us and challenged us to continue to keep pursuing oneness, not only in ministry but also in our home.

On the drive home that day, we were deeply encouraged. As we reflected on where we started, in a relationship that was emotionally broken, we began to praise God for His work. Any oneness that Bob and Pat saw was a credit to the saving work of Christ alone.

God continues to affirm our growth in oneness, encouraging us forward. Once while visiting New York City, we decided to catch an Uber from our hotel to the Empire State Building. Our talkative driver asked if this was a vacation and if we had ever been to New York City before. We told him yes to both and then said that normally we come to New York for ministry-related work and had never visited just as tourists. This was, we shared, a weekend to break away from the California sunshine and enjoy the New York City snow and cold weeks before Christmas.

As we talked about starting a new church in North Long Beach, California, our driver began to ask what it looked like for a family to serve together in ministry. That question ultimately allowed us to share the gospel message with him. D. A. and I were going back and forth, talking about Scripture, life experiences, and our gratitude to the Lord.

To our surprise, the driver suddenly cut us off: "I'm really encouraged by how you two act together," he said. "You're really in sync when you talk. You have what other people spend their lives trying to find." We were floored. We told him we were grateful for his words but that we give all praise to God because we are not always on the same page—and in fact, that we've walked through a lot of brokenness in our marriage. This brought us back to the gospel. The Good News reminds us that God can take our brokenness and make it something beautiful. As we surrender our brokenness to God, He builds us together into one. This is a gospel-saturated marriage.

Seeing the work that God has done in our lives, and our marriage, spurs us to continue to pursue greater depths of oneness. God has done incredible things with our brokenness—and He can do the same in your marriage. Even if you feel as though you and your spouse are far apart, God is mighty enough to see you, mighty enough to salvage your marriage, and mighty enough to help you progress toward greater levels of oneness together. The gospel carries the omnipotent power of God (Romans 1:16-17). He has the power to make two people become one, unified in heart and in mission.

CHAPTER 3

CAN WE TALK?

Let no corrupting talk come out of your mouths, but only such as is good for building up, as fits the occasion, that it may give grace to those who hear.

EPHESIANS 4:29

Elicia

Change begins with a conversation. With our words we can build up or destroy the spirits of people. Proverbs 18:20-21 says, "From the fruit of a man's mouth his stomach is satisfied; he is satisfied by the yield of his lips. Death and life are in the power of the tongue, and those who love it will eat its fruits." Our words have power, although that power is limited when compared to the sovereignty of God. Nothing we can say can thwart His plan. But the things we say do carry consequences, both positive and negative.

Spouses are guaranteed to have breakdowns in communication. Life gets hectic after the honeymoon, and when cell phones, jobs, and children are competing for our attention, shutting down tends to keep us from blowing up! Yet, to have gospel-saturated marriages, we need genuine communication. And even though it's often a fight just to get time alone to talk, the rewards outweigh the struggle.

Communication Breakdown

Pastor David Moore said the average couple spends thirty-seven minutes a week in meaningful, private communication.[1] That's only about five minutes of talking per day—no worthwhile relationship can survive on that! And this statistic is from years before current technology hit the markets. Many marriages are skating on thin ice because of a lack of communication, which is a direct result of the busyness of life.

In his book *That Crazy Little Thing Called Love*, Jud Wilhite says, "The greatest threat to our marriages and families today is not financial problems, or infidelity, or the state of the Union. The greatest threat is busyness."[2] Busyness tends to mutate our homes into environments where everything is touch and go. We assume we are communicating when really we're just exchanging factual information about our days and unfinished tasks that need to be completed. Married couples who endure this process drift apart over time and begin to look at each other more as roommates than as husband and wife.

Research shows that the happiest couples are those who share their hopes, dreams, and fears with each other.[3] Communication in a marriage should be holistic—not limited to everyday tasks that need to be completed, but extending to the content of each spouse's heart. When one spouse shares from a vulnerable place, the other must work to listen and engage with what was shared. In our marriage, our process of communication is damaged when I share the content of my heart and D. A. just stares at me with a blank look, doesn't respond, or changes the subject. Such experiences tempt me to remain guarded with my feelings and to keep things on a task-oriented surface level. Our words and actions are linked, so if I choose to remain selfish by not sharing my heart with D. A., I will become selfish in my actions toward him as well. A gospel-saturated marriage fights for consistent holistic communication, which leads to selfless living.

Shutting down the lines of communication can quickly lead to behavior patterns that carry the potential to damage or destroy a marriage. Dr. John Gottman has identified four behavior patterns that have caused him to accurately predict divorces in couples. He calls these patterns "the Four Horsemen of the Apocalypse": criticism, contempt, defensiveness, and stonewalling.[4] Each of these patterns involves high levels of selfishness, name-calling, blame shifting, and emotional withdrawal. These patterns thrive in environments where holistic communication is not practiced.

Communication, or lack thereof, can either make or break a marriage. Being a Christian does not exempt a person from being a poor communicator; we all must be diligent to communicate with our spouses in such a way that we're understanding each other more than fighting to be understood. As

Christians, we are careful with our language when we steward God's Word because we want to communicate the heart of our God rightly. Yet we often fail to use clear and descriptive language when speaking to our spouses. (At least, that's our struggle in the Horton household.) Men and women are different, and the ways in which we think, speak, and act are different, which is why we need to use precise language. Being intentional with our words helps our spouses understand what we're saying.

Clear communication plays a key role in creating oneness in marriage, particularly as you're developing your own family culture. As we talked about in the last chapter, you cannot develop your own family rhythm and traditions if you're always resorting back to what your family practiced when you were growing up. D. A. and I now see how communication (or lack thereof) affected our struggle to find our identity of oneness during our early years of marriage.

One Sunday afternoon, we headed home after church to chill and unwind. I went into the kitchen to find something to cook for lunch. As I opened the fridge, I suddenly remembered that my mom had told me she would be making a big pot of spaghetti after church and that we were welcome to come over to eat and watch football. Cue the celebration music! I didn't have to cook, and Mom was making spaghetti! Her sauce is amazing—it's worth canceling all plans just to partake in that heavenly goodness. So it was a no-brainer for me.

I rushed into the other room and told D. A., "My mom is making spaghetti!" He gave me a blank stare and nodded.

"That's good," he said. Time stood still as I waited for a further response. I had been sure he would match my enthusiasm by marching right back upstairs, changing his church clothes, and putting on something a little more comfortable and stretchy. (In case you were wondering, Mom's spaghetti equals the need for stretchy pants.)

He then asked, "So what are you making for lunch?" At that, a war started raging deep in my soul. I tried to muster the self-control to not show my disgust and spew out a sarcastic remark. I wanted to lovingly remind my sweet husband that I wasn't planning on making lunch and that it was a grand idea for us to make the trip to my parents' house for Sunday lunch. Instead, I opened my mouth and said, "Seriously, are you kidding me?"

I stormed out of the kitchen, walked right upstairs, and plunged my face into a pillow, crying in frustration and despair. I wish I could say the story ended well, but it didn't.

It wasn't until months later that we finally discussed what happened. My sweet husband hadn't realized that I was trying to clue him in to my desire to go to my parents' house for spaghetti. I indeed said that my mom was making spaghetti, and in his mind he heard a statement, not a question, which he acknowledged with "That's good." I never asked him if he wanted to go. I had assumed he would just pick up on my meaning, and when he didn't, I assumed wrong motives in his response. (Calling him a jerk-face didn't help the situation either.)

Communication is integral for oneness in marriage. As

much as D. A. and I like to think that we'll eventually learn how to read each other's minds, it's not going to happen. Both of us need to put forth the effort to keep the lines of communication open.

Here's a simple principle to keep in mind: Assumptions lead to more assumptions, and communication leads to more communication. It's never healthy to assume that the person you are trying to communicate with understands your heart unless you have shared your heart. Assumptions about what someone does or doesn't understand simply create assumptions about that person's response. The best way you can avoid the confusion that assumptions bring is to use clear and honest communication that invites your spouse to respond with open communication in return.

Now, there's a caveat to this: Sometimes you'll express what's on your heart, but your spouse isn't ready to handle it. Don't retreat. Don't close up shop. Keep the light on. Pray hard. And instead of always praying for God to change the other person, begin by praying that God will first change your heart. Transformation begins with you. You can't expect your spouse to miraculously be ready to listen to your heart, but God is always ready. Any lack of communication between your spouse and you should push you into deeper communication with our heavenly Father. As James 4:8 says, "Draw near to God, and he will draw near to you."

The best communication between spouses, though, is always reciprocal. In the bestselling book *Men Are from Mars, Women Are from Venus*, author John Gray highlights this relational truth: "When a man can listen to a woman's feelings without getting angry and frustrated, he gives her a wonderful gift. He makes it safe for her to express herself. The more she is able to express herself, the more she feels heard and understood, and the more she is able to give a man the loving trust, acceptance, appreciation, admiration, approval and encouragement that he needs."[5]

Boom! This nugget of truth gives us a framework for constructing our lines of communication. Reciprocity gives both people a foundation to build on. If a woman is feeling heard, she feels safe and secure. The vulnerability of her heart that she so desperately desires to share with her husband will not fall on deaf ears, and vice versa.

The nonverbal aspect of communication—and how we respond to those nonverbal cues—plays an important role in reciprocity as well. Someone's body language can make us want to immediately tune that person out. Or if someone's tone is disrespectful, we can be quick to disregard his or her feelings and fight back with ugliness. Tone and body language—from both sides!—can make or break healthy communication. Who wants to listen to someone scream at the top of his or her lungs? If you're yelling at me, I may be prone to yell right back to be heard. But the heart of the matter never really gets discussed.

These communication struggles, to one degree or another, happen in *all* homes—even Christian homes! So to learn how to communicate better and resolve conflict effectively, we're going to get practical. You can have strong and healthy communication in your marriage—if you and your spouse are intentional about equipping yourselves and act on what you've learned.

The Levels of Communication

D. A.

Let's start with something foundational: What does communication look like? Elicia and I have always found John Powell's five levels of communication helpful in our marriage.[6] These levels range from the most superficial (level five) to the most transparent and vulnerable (level one):

> *Level five* is the world of clichés, where conversation feels the safest. Personal feelings and emotions are hidden behind superficial phrases. This level is all about self-preservation. You can see this level in action when someone is noticeably offended but, when asked about his or her feelings, responds with "I'm fine." That person wants the conversation to stay at level five.

> *Level four* is the news reporter. This is where information is exchanged with no emotion. An example of this level is when one spouse asks the other about his or her day and the spouse responds with the facts and no personal commentary.

> *Level three* is when someone begins to open up by sharing personal ideas. This level is often a way of testing the

water to see if it's safe to share more. Powell says that if the spouse who receives the information rejects what his or her spouse is communicating, the spouse who is sharing will likely retreat to level four or even five.

Level two is when someone starts to share emotions and feelings, beginning to unveil his or her heart. Sadly, for the first five years of our marriage, Elicia and I rarely got to this level of communication. It took a move of God in both of us to help us finally trust each other with our entire hearts, opening the door to level one communication.

Level one is when there is complete emotional and personal communication. This level involves full vulnerability. No information is off-limits; childhood experiences and secrets can be discovered and exposed. At this level, every barrier of self-preservation has been taken down. However, it's both impossible and unwise to operate, or strive to be, at this level all the time. Spouses should access this level during specific times to avoid interruptions.

Elicia and I got to level one for the first time at a church-planting boot camp in Jefferson City, Missouri. After the teaching ended at 9:00 p.m., all of us were challenged to go back to our hotel rooms to talk through the vision we had for our marriages in relation to the churches we were going to plant. In the morning at breakfast we'd give a short presentation on what we discussed.

Initially, Elicia and I started out at level three, discussing strategies of evangelism, team building for the launch, and issues that were going on in the church. As the night progressed, we found ourselves unpacking our fears and reservations about planting the church in the middle of the neighbor*hood* (emphasis on *hood*) that Elicia had been raised in. Around 1:00 a.m., we found ourselves overtaken by the desire to tear down every wall of self-preservation, to share anything and everything that came to mind, to ask about things we wanted to know but never had the guts to ask.

It was during this time that Elicia shared about being molested at the age of seven. Every emotion imaginable was visible between us in that moment. She felt a level of embarrassment as she related the details through tears. I was angry that she had been victimized and upset that I hadn't been there to protect her. I was the first person she had ever told— she had been a prisoner of that secret for nearly twenty years. I felt privileged that she would share this information, and at the same time I felt her pain and hated seeing her so broken.

There was a long pause in the conversation. Deafening silence filled the room; the only sound was occasional weeping. This was the most intimate connection we had ever had. When she was ready, Elicia began speaking again, this time expressing her remorse for keeping me at a distance when I pursued her sexually. Because she hadn't been able to share or process her victimization fully, residual effects complicated our marriage. She said that certain ways I would touch her made her skin crawl because it felt similar to when she was a child.

She confided that whenever I tried to romance her and get her in the mood, she had an internal wrestling match going on in her heart and mind. Part of her was saying, *It's okay to give myself to my husband because he is my husband.* But the other part of her was the scared child who would freeze because she didn't understand what was going on.

When she would reject my advances, I was borderline depressed. I would lie next to her in bed, engaged in my own mental warfare, feeling she wasn't attracted to me and almost convincing myself that she was cheating on me. My insecurities began to hold me hostage. We didn't know the depth of each other's struggles, and the main reason we remained in the dark was because we weren't talking to each other about what we were enduring.

Getting to the most intimate levels of communication is vital for a healthy marriage because vulnerability gives both spouses the opportunity to live selflessly instead of selfishly. Selfless living empowers the gospel-saturated marriage, strengthening each spouse to remain courageous in pursuing deeper communication.

The Communication of Love Languages

Elicia

One reason my rejection hurt D. A. so deeply was because his primary love language is physical touch, and his secondary love language is words of affirmation. When I struggled to show any physical interest or provide him with any kind of verbal affirmation, he felt doubly rejected. I, on the other hand, hear "I love you" not through words or sexual intimacy but through D. A. intentionally carving out quality time for us to be together and serving me. One of the biggest communication hurdles we had to overcome was becoming fluent in or, as Dr. Gary Chapman says, *mastering*[7] the other's love language.

For those who are not familiar with Dr. Gary Chapman's book *The Five Love Languages*,[8] allow us the privilege of providing you with a brief overview. Dr. Chapman says that there are five ways people normally hear "I love you." Here are the five love languages, contextualized to a marital relationship:

1. *Words of affirmation.* This person hears "I love you" every time his or her spouse expresses gratitude (e.g., "I appreciate you," "You did an excellent job," "Thank you for all you do"). This person feels *rejected* when his or her spouse offers nonconstructive criticism or ignores contributions.

2. *Quality time.* This person hears "I love you" every time his or her spouse carves out space for focused and personal attention (e.g., a candlelit dinner at home, a date night, a weekend getaway). This person feels *rejected* when the relationship becomes touch and go (e.g., "hello and good-bye," "we seem more like roommates").

3. *Receiving gifts.* This person hears "I love you" every time his or her spouse gives a gift that carries strong

sentimental value or indicates careful thought—perhaps a "Thinking of You" card, a toy reminiscent of their childhood, or a bouquet of flowers. This person feels *rejected* when special occasions are forgotten (e.g., anniversaries, birthdays, and other sentimental occasions).

4. *Acts of service.* This person hears "I love you" every time his or her spouse helps carry out responsibilities (e.g., chores, finances, home decorating projects). This person feels *rejected* when his or her spouse ignores needs at home yet makes time to serve and meet the needs of others.

5. *Physical touch.* This person hears "I love you" every time his or her spouse makes physical contact (e.g., an embrace, hand-holding, a passionate kiss, sexual intimacy). This person feels *rejected* when physically neglected or abused.

Frustrations will likely occur in your marriage if you try to say "I love you" in your own love language instead of your spouse's. It's almost like approaching someone on the street and asking him or her for directions, only to be met with an awkward smile and blank stare. As you probe further, the person makes a hand motion, indicating a language barrier. The same could be said of D. A. and me early in our marriage, and even still to this day. There are times when D. A. shuts down and becomes emotionally distant from me just because

I haven't acknowledged him after he's given me numerous compliments. I normally say thank you, but D. A. is really asking for more—for me to affirm him verbally! I don't usually pick up on the hint because his intent isn't clear.

On the flip side, sometimes months went by without us having a date night, and it never seemed to bother D. A. I felt guilty for even bringing it up because of his traveling schedule and how deeply invested he was in the pastorate and seminary. At times it seemed as though he only wanted to be alone with me when he desired sexual intimacy, and I felt that he didn't pursue me outside of that. When I would mention it to him, he would go from zero to one hundred in pursuit of me to make up for lost time. Then he would run out of gas, and things went back to the way they were before I broke my silence.

This was the normal tension in the Horton household for the first ten years of our marriage—including five years after we finally delved into Powell's level one communication. And we still revisit tension every now and then. Choosing to remain alert to and intentional about each other's love language is critical as we face every aspect of marriage—and it helps us as D. A. and I discern how best to resolve conflict.

D. A.
Conflict Resolution
Learning to communicate in times of conflict is crucial for a healthy marriage. It's easy to assume that conflict is a bad thing and try to avoid it, but conflict is not inherently bad.

In fact, conflict is a great tool that digs up past hurts and brokenness so that couples can confront them and find true healing.

Healthy communication is how conflict can be resolved in marriage. Resolving conflict is different from avoiding or managing conflict. When we avoided conflict, we suppressed our pain until we'd blow up and have an argument that lasted for hours, followed by days of uneasiness. Managing conflict meant that we were putting Band-Aid solutions on gaping heart wounds that were becoming infected with bitterness. But there is a better way to manage conflict in a Christian marriage.

FEAR

To successfully engage in healthy conflict resolution, you must first identify the ways in which you and your spouse deal with anger and disappointment. Often, anger stems from fear. Thinking of conflict in terms of the acronym FEAR will help you identify the four ways in which you might respond to your spouse when angry or disappointed:

Fight: making verbal attacks with trigger words used to hurt your spouse; digging up past issues to justify anger

Escape: avoiding the conversation and issue by either refusing to talk about it, changing the topic, or simply walking away with no intention of coming back and discussing the issue

Apathy: responding as if you don't care or saying nothing to further upset your spouse

Resolve: taking time to locate the root issue of the argument, bringing it to the forefront of the conversation, and working to find a resolution

In marriage, many arguments involve only the first three responses. When one person lashes out, the other retaliates, eventually leading to a shouting match and one spouse doing or saying something drastic. This has certainly been true in our marriage. We are still God's work in progress!

Elicia

There I was, seven months pregnant, standing in the middle of our living room and watching my husband undress himself. Prior to that moment, I had gathered a bag of personal belongings and a fistful of Kleenexes. I was headed out the door.

Our honeymoon phase had ended pretty quickly when a month after our wedding we discovered we had a souvenir from Florida: a baby in my belly.

I was so emotional, thinking of all the responsibilities of being a new wife *and* mom while working full-time and being in school. I had been fooling myself, thinking I could keep this juggling act going while D. A. ran his own circus. (Yes, he, too, was a circus act.) D. A. was walking a tightrope, juggling ten different things with no net to catch him. He was trying to convince me the Lord was leading him to Bible college—while he also served as a pastor, traveled to rap, and waited tables at Lone Star Steakhouse.

That was our life. At twenty-one and twenty-three years old, we found ourselves living in constant spiritual immaturity—neither of us had been biblically discipled because the Lord had saved us in our teenage years.

I was aimless. I had no compass and was too prideful to admit it. So, like a lost driver refusing to pull over and ask for directions, I dismissed the idea of asking God for a little help.

I was just gonna keep driving on fumes, hoping to make it to the nearest exit. A quick exit out of my current circumstances. The easy way out. The path of least resistance.

That night in our living room, I tried explaining that I needed time to think. D. A. agreed but insisted we think through things together. I disagreed.

Very politely I told him that our thinking stunk and I'd rather get away to reflect. I was so sick of us fussing over plans for our future. I figured that once the baby arrived, I'd have somewhat of an idea. He, on the other hand, was all over the place with his plans and goals. We weren't on the same page at all. (Mind you, we had been married only eight months.)

In retrospect, my heart wasn't prepared to see D. A. fall off his tightrope. If he was supposed to lead and shepherd me, then he was off to a bad start. And, to be quite honest, I didn't know what true love meant. Plus, D. A. and I were extremely undisciplined in our walks with God. We didn't spend any time reading the Bible or praying together—or praying for each other. Here we were upgrading to an SUV, buying baby clothes, and playing house. Getting married and having kids will make you grow up *real quick*, but it won't help you grow spiritually if you keep leaving God out of the equation.

We both stood in the middle of the living room, in a fight in which nobody made sense. I was getting heated because he wouldn't let me just leave. I couldn't think of anything else to say until I said it—the words I never thought I would hear come out of my mouth: "I'm done!"

Silence.

I couldn't press rewind or pause for station identification. He had heard it clearly, and I know now that the words pierced him to the core.

Then it happened.

He snapped. He lost it. I knew he would never lay his hands on me, but in case he were to attempt anything, I was ready to pull a ninja move: forward roll my pregnant belly across the living room floor and grab the knife that was chilling on the kitchen counter. I am from the hood, homie, and I know how to take it to the streets if necessary.

I was trying to figure out an escape plan while he was stomping and yelling out, "Oh, you're gonna leave me now?" Then suddenly, out of nowhere, he stopped, stood still, looked me right in the eyes, and calmly opened the front door. And then the unthinkable happened.

He started taking off his clothes. He slid off his size 3X Phat Farm hoodie, pulled his XXL-Tall T-shirt over his head, and removed his undershirt. Then he moved right along to his oversized jeans. And boots.

He was nearly butt naked—down to just his boxers and socks. And I lost it. All I could do was laugh. He literally could not think of anything else to do to grab my attention and deactivate an intense situation.

"What's wrong?" he asked me, as if he weren't standing almost nude with the front door wide open for all the neighbors to see. I had no words. We both had just experienced a mixture of despair, psychosis, humor, and pregnant-lady hormones in a matter of minutes. All we could do was laugh.

He turned to me again and said, "Through all of this we have not even cried out to God and asked for His help. Can we just stop and pray?"

He was right. We had never once stopped to fully depend on the one whom we professed as Lord of our lives to help us in our desperate time of need.

During our courtship, we both flippantly professed our love for each other but never truly understood its fullness or spiritual implications. At no time did we completely grasp this passage in 1 Corinthians 13: "Love is patient and kind; love does not envy or boast; it is not arrogant or rude. It does not insist on its own way; it is not irritable or resentful; it does not rejoice at wrongdoing, but rejoices with the truth. Love bears *all* things, believes *all* things, hopes *all* things, endures *all* things. Love never ends" (verses 4-8, emphasis added).

We didn't know what real love was. Even more so, we didn't realize the power of the Holy Spirit, who would help us crucify our fleshly desires to hurt each other and forsake our vows. We were so quick to "take it back to the streets" that we never once fully relied on God in *all* things. That day has helped us bring glory to God in so many ways.

This story, which we were once too embarrassed to even speak about, has helped so many couples through premarital and marriage counseling. God has helped us learn to appreciate the extremely difficult times—the times that allow raw feelings to surface. We've seen each other at our worst; yet the gospel compels us to keep on loving each other as God first loved us. Ultimately, love does endure *all* things.

If you want God to be at the center of your marriage, make sure you work to keep Him there, not leaving Him in the trunk like a spare tire, only to be taken out whenever you get a flat. In our marriage, we both have come to realize that spiritual growth and maturity help us love each other deeply, despite our flaws and lapses of judgment.

While it is important to invest and plan for your future together, it is even more important to invest in your spiritual growth as individuals. By doing so, you can truly give your spouse the best he or she deserves.

Marriage is hard work. It takes sacrifice. When our spouses strip off their clothes or want to walk out the door, remember love believes *all* things, hopes *all* things, and endures *all* things—because love never ends. So get to work. Roll up those sleeves, put your pants back on, and fight back with prayer.

Sound romantic? Not really. I wish we could say this was the only time we had such a blowup, but that's not the case.

D. A.

Elicia had spent most of the day preparing a nice meal, including her famous made-from-scratch lasagna, for a couple we were having over for a marriage counseling session that evening. The kids and I cleaned the house while Elicia cooked, but we had to frequently stop our daughters from bickering.

An hour before the couple's scheduled arrival, tensions mounted, and Elicia and I started making sarcastic comments to each other. Then, all of a sudden, Elicia said she was tired of being in a loveless marriage. I lost it! I stopped washing the dishes, slammed my fist on the counter, said, "I'm done with you," and walked out of the house, slamming the door behind me.

It was November in Kansas City, so it was cold. All I had on were jeans, boots, and a hoodie. Initially I was so upset that the cold didn't bother me, but as time went on and I walked farther around our neighborhood, I got very cold. My pride kept me from going back and working things out with Elicia. I kept walking up and down the main street we lived near. When I couldn't take the cold anymore, I walked back to our house, opened the front door (which Elicia graciously kept unlocked), and went into our bedroom. Elicia came in a few minutes later and said she had canceled the counseling session with the other couple. We, she told me, needed to work on *our* issues.

We talked for the next thirty minutes and determined that the root cause of our fight was fear. Elicia had been afraid that she wouldn't have enough time to get herself ready to host. And rather than trying to resolve her fear, she chose to fight with me by saying we had a loveless marriage. Because I thought she might leave, I then responded in fear, deciding to walk out first—beating her to the punch. We were both wrong. After we confessed our sins, forgave each other, repented, and prayed, we asked our kids for their forgiveness as well.

The next day we pulled the couple aside after church and told them about our fight and how embarrassed we were. When they heard what had happened, they laughed and said they'd had a bad argument and were also going to cancel. They let us know how much they appreciated being counseled by a pastor and his wife who fought and made it a point to let others know they're not alone in the struggle.

The Four Nevers

Over the course of our marriage, we've identified some helpful strategies for dealing with the conflicts we face. Sometimes we pray and try to determine what caused us to continue to be combative in our speech. From our experiences, we've developed what we call the Four Nevers. When either one of us responds to a tense conversation with the urge to fight, escape, or act apathetic, we use the Four Nevers as a way to work toward resolution. Consider using these in your own marriage:

1. *Never Fight Back.* Even if one of you desires to fight, the other should communicate that he or she is going to walk away from the conversation. This allows each

of you to pray and gather your thoughts with the intention of coming back to resolve the issue. This is a very challenging practice to develop as a habit; however, it can prevent you from going head-to-head and allows God to speak directly to your hearts.

2. *Never Avoid the Issues.* Rabbit trails will take you further away from the issue that is putting you at odds. Both of you should work diligently to take the conversation toward level two. If you have the opportunity to be without interruption, consider diving as deep as level one.

3. *Never Act As Though You Don't Care.* Both of you honestly do care for your spouse's emotional well-being and the overall health of the relationship. However, when either of you is operating in the flesh, you will be less likely to remain sensitive to your spouse's wounds. Acting as if you don't care will only add insult to the injuries already caused.

4. *Never Use Manipulation to Get Your Way.* We're all guilty of manipulating arguments to get what we really want. If you do this, however, you're preventing your spouse from getting what he or she wanted. Here are a few manipulative practices to avoid: saying "I'm sorry" just to end the argument, denying that there is an issue and acting as though your spouse is crazy and making up a problem, and acting as though you're not bothered so your spouse will no longer be bothered.

Our disagreements and differing vantage points weren't what drove us to develop the Four Nevers. Early in our marriage, Elicia and I missed multiple opportunities to grow deeper in our walk together by resolving conflict in a biblical manner. The words we used created a great stumbling block in developing a deeper sense of togetherness. Our conversations were laced with bitterness, personal attacks, and trigger words. We were prone to go head-to-head for hours before we started using the Four Nevers.

In fact, we sat down and developed the Four Nevers because we were tired of *fighting*. We were convicted as we studied Ephesians 4:29, which says, "Let no corrupting talk come out of your mouths, but only such as is good for building up, as fits the occasion, that it may give grace to those who hear."

Conflict in a long-term relationship is inevitable. In fact, healthy conflict can be a litmus test for a marriage because its presence or lack thereof can measure how superficial the relationship is. Conflict is not damaging in and of itself, but words can be.

Corrupt talk is both foul and harmful. The Greek word translated as "corrupt," *sapros*, was often used to describe spoiled meat. Before Elicia and I were married, I accidently left a cooked Cornish hen in the trunk of my car. After two weeks, the stench was so bad that I had to pull over, get out of the car, and open the trunk to see what was causing the foul smell. I found the Cornish hen decomposing and filled with maggots.

This is what our words become when we argue in

damaging ways. Corrupt talk is as beneficial to a relationship as that maggot-filled Cornish hen.

Rather than speaking that kind of filth, couples should use speech that builds up. In Ephesians, Paul describes language that edifies those we're speaking with. Edification includes constructive criticism given in humility, allowing the person receiving those words to correct behavior that's not conducive for togetherness. When we use such speech, Paul says we will "give grace to those who hear." This is a very important phrase because it identifies an audience beyond the people we are talking to. For married couples, this audience can be our very own children!

Recognizing this truth in our own marriage caused our hearts to break. For years we had been showing our children all the ways to *not* resolve conflict. They were casualties of the wars we were fighting with each other. We knew that we disagreed with how our parents managed conflict, yet we were guilty of repeating many of their patterns. We were convicted to the point we knew we had to confess our sins (to our children as well as to each other), identify where we were getting off course, and develop strategies for resolving our conflicts biblically.

IDEAL

Elicia
When we realized that our behavior during times of conflict needed to change radically, we created a practical five-step process using the acrostic IDEAL, which reflected our ideal

way of resolving our issues. These principles may look a little different in your marriage, but if you're struggling with yielding to the Holy Spirit during times of conflict, prayerfully consider trying these five practices:

It's Okay to Walk Away. It's good to remind each other that it's perfectly acceptable to walk away when things get overheated. Call a time-out and agree to be apart for a set amount of time. During this time, pray and ask God for grace and patience for when you come back together to seek resolution.

Define the Problem. When you reconvene, take time to identify what you each sense is the root cause of your disagreement. Sometimes you'll both agree on what triggered the dispute, and other times you won't. Both of you must be willing to hear the other person's assessment in order to tackle all the issues that might be preventing you from walking in togetherness. Any stated root problems need to be addressed.

Examine your own heart. Take the time necessary to ask the Lord to highlight your blind spots by reading and praying through Psalm 139:23-24. In addition, ask the Lord to prepare your heart to hear your spouse share the blind spots they see in your life.

Actively Listen to Your Spouse. When both of you are demanding to be heard, neither one of you is taking time to listen. Consider opening the Bible, reading the following Scriptures, and asking God the Holy Spirit to help both of you become better listeners:

> Proverbs 15:1: "A soft answer turns away wrath, but a harsh word stirs up anger."
>
> Proverbs 18:13: "If one gives an answer before he hears, it is his folly and shame."
>
> James 1:19-20: "Know this, my beloved brothers: let every person be quick to hear, slow to speak, slow to anger; for the anger of man does not produce the righteousness of God."

List Your Contributions and Solutions. In most cases, both spouses contribute something to the stated problem or problems, so each of you must equally contribute to finding a solution rather than just harping on the other person's faults.

Once we started employing this strategy, we saw immediate results, as did our children. Our knock-down, drag-out fights began to decrease. We spent increased time working through issues while expressing empathy and sympathy. We no longer raised our voices with each other—to the point that when we did during one silly spat about dinner, our oldest daughter started to cry. When I asked why she was crying, Bella told us she was worried we would get a divorce. Immediately D. A. and I looked at each other, puzzled, and asked why she assumed that. Bella said it was because D. A.

had raised his voice when he told me he didn't care what we ate.

We quickly told her we were not getting divorced and assured her of our love. Then we asked her how often we raised our voices or even fought. Bella couldn't remember one other occurrence. We found this comforting. The Lord was honoring our commitment to biblical resolution—to the point that our oldest daughter, who had witnessed many of our earlier altercations, could no longer remember the way we used to fight! If you and your spouse struggle with conflict resolution, be encouraged: If God can cause growth in us, He can do it in anyone.

Social Media and Texting

D. A.

We would be remiss if we didn't address one final key issue when it comes to communication in marriage: how social media and texting affect households. Communication using technology is not inherently bad, but it must fit within a framework that benefits a marriage rather than burdens it.

Younger generations are more prone to use social media and technology as a means of communicating and connecting. In one recent study, 41 percent of eighteen- to twenty-nine-year-olds in marriages or committed relationships felt closer to their partners because of social media and texting. Yet 42 percent said their partners were regularly distracted by their cell phones, compared to 25 percent of all who were surveyed. Each age group reported the way they handle conflict has changed because of technology. Overall, 9 percent said they had resolved an argument online or over text message, compared to 23 percent in the eighteen- to twenty-nine-year-old range. Online engagement is also a cause for contention in relationships. In the eighteen- to twenty-nine age group, 18 percent said they had argued with their partner about the amount of time he or she spends online, compared to 8 percent across all age groups.[9]

Elicia and I were newly dating around the time text messaging hit the market. This was back in the day when it cost twenty-five cents to send a text message and ten cents to receive one. We texted each other a lot, and—since I'm being transparent—most of our arguments bled into back-and-forth text wars. One month I racked up a $1,200 bill. Yes—$1,200! Fortunately, over the years we have matured. Technology is most beneficial to relationships when it is not a point of contention but rather a way to track family and personal situations throughout the day.

Positive Uses

Elicia
Technology can provide vulnerability and transparency in a marriage, if both spouses agree to use it in ways that help rather than harm their relationship. In our marriage, we wanted to be proactive in developing accountability with every form of technology we use, so we shared the passwords

for every online account we have and the passwords for our cell phones. We each reserve the right to look through the other person's phone and social media accounts (including in-boxes) at any time and ask any questions about comments or messages. When you truly have nothing to hide, giving your password to your spouse is no problem.

We leverage technology to work better together as parents as well. We often text each other when we don't want our kids to know what we're talking about, whether it's surprising them with dinner out or needing to speak to them in real time about an issue. Sometimes D. A. will text to remind me that we need to address a harsh comment from one of our kids. Or if something comes on TV that causes us to change the channel, I may text D. A. to suggest maximizing the moment by explaining why the scene was inappropriate.

Another benefit of technology in marriage is that it allows a couple to demonstrate the strength of their marriage to a watching world. Once, an ex-girlfriend of D. A.'s asked to be his friend on Facebook, and I was bothered because I felt that she wouldn't have tried to connect if his social media offered better evidence of the health of our marriage. I wrestled with how to ask D. A. to show our togetherness more consistently online. When we were able to steal away for our first date night in months, I gently brought up my concerns. D. A. apologized, and to this day he is warm and intentional about how he talks about our marriage online.

A couple should also be intentional about communicating the importance of their marriage to other people, even when marriage is hard. D. A. once posted a picture when we were not getting along—we'd had a rough morning, were running on limited sleep, and were frustrated with each other. We had just boarded a plane and were about to take off when suddenly D. A. pulled out his phone and said he was going to take our picture.

I was upset and told him I wasn't going to participate. He reminded me of our commitment and said that if we show people only the good times, we are hypocrites. All of life, and especially all of marriage, is not always good. He wanted the world to see that even in our togetherness and ministry we don't always get along. God is still working on us.

D. A. captioned the picture, "Truth be told, it's been a rough morning. Yet Romans 8:9-13 gives us the reassurance [that] God the Holy Spirit provides us with strength to put to death the misdeeds of our flesh."

Negative Uses

Now, we have to be honest: Technology has also had a negative impact on our marriage. Sometimes we use text messages to avoid talking about a concern in person. It's easier to text because it completely removes the complications of body language and tone. For us, speaking in emojis can be easier than speaking face-to-face. We've had to learn to not let text messaging replace face-to-face time when we're dealing with hard conversations.

We dealt with this as we were going through the church-planting process. The Lord called our family to plant a church in California, and we were in the middle of trying to find areas that would provide a soft landing for our family and give us time to get acclimated. We and the other two couples on the team felt led to plant the church in south LA County, which includes places such as Carson, Long Beach, Lakewood, Bellflower . . . and Compton. And because most people aren't familiar with that area, they automatically assume that south LA County equals *Straight Outta Compton*. Soon, word began to circulate that we were going to Compton to plant a church.

When I caught wind of this, I was so upset that my loving husband was now telling people that we were indeed planting a church in Compton. But we had never decided on Compton as a team—we hadn't yet discerned which specific city we should go to! Despite the turmoil about this, we continued to avoid the conversation.

Everything came to a head one day as we talked with the other leaders via GroupMe (a group text app) about exactly which city we felt God wanted us to reach. D. A. and I were literally in the same small apartment, less than twenty feet apart, both on our phones. In a group message, D. A. brought up the idea of Long Beach, which had never been a city either one of us had felt led to pray about.

We both knew the choice of city was a point of contention, which is why we were both fine with employing complete avoidance. We were using technology to avoid addressing sore spots the Lord wanted us to talk about in order to bring us back to a sense of oneness.

This kind of distance happens to all of us. We have become so dependent on technology for communication that we often fail to really connect one-on-one with people and allow our real feelings to be shared and discussed. Text messages, e-mails, and social media dialogues can easily be misinterpreted and misconstrued. We use emojis rather than relaying our true emotions. We are quick to FaceTime but aren't good about carving out time for real face time.

I love technology and its capabilities, but we need to be cautious. It can become such a hindrance if not used with proper care and discipline.

Technology can also have a negative impact when a couple allows it to distract them from engaging and being present with each other and their kids. One time when D. A. and I went out to eat at a restaurant, we noticed a family of five sitting at a table directly across from us. All of them were on their personal electronic devices. The only time they looked up from their devices was to order their food.

Afterward, our family said we hoped we'd never be like that. But then we remembered how many times we have eaten dinner together at home with computers, cell phones, and iPads holding our attention hostage. Hypocrisy at its finest! How can we judge another family for doing in public what we are often guilty of doing in private? From that moment we recognized we were in error and sought to ban all electronic devices from the dinner table.

Technology is both a blessing and a curse—a blessing because it allows couples to communicate while they are away from each other, and a curse because it is competing for their attention. Gospel-saturated marriages seek to leverage technology for the benefit of togetherness in the household. And at the same time, gospel-saturated marriages allow other families to develop their own convictions.

The Goal of Communication

Communication in a gospel-saturated marriage should foster such togetherness that other couples who witness it will want the same. Imagine if the watching world saw couples consistently communicating "I love you" in their spouses' heart language. The world would truly be amazed by how well these couples knew each other's needs and how they took the time to steward their spouses' hearts and vulnerability.

Gospel-saturated marriages can become billboards for authentic relationships and encourage other marriages by demonstrating clear and vulnerable communication, application of Scripture during times of conflict, healthy and honoring conflict resolution, and use of technology that builds up families.

Practices that foster genuine accountability between spouses will help safeguard marriages from distractions and temptations. Accountability happens when truthful communication is coupled with transparent living. Biblical communication leads to greater depths of togetherness in the lifelong commitment of marriage, with God as our center, allowing Christ to anchor our souls when we find ourselves in rough seas.

CHAPTER 4

GOING THE DISTANCE

I consider that the sufferings of this present time are not worth comparing with the glory that is to be revealed to us.

ROMANS 8:18

Elicia

Suffering is an unavoidable reality because we all live in a fallen world cursed by sin. And suffering can make or break a relationship. D. A. and I have endured some hard seasons in our marriage—the death of loved ones, health struggles, conflicts between our families, and issues in churches where we were either leaders or members. You have undoubtedly faced suffering in your marriage as well. The world seeks to destroy our marriages. But we've learned that when spouses cling to God and each other during seasons of suffering, the anguish can bring them closer together instead of ripping them apart.

For nearly two years, D. A. and I felt like we were getting hit from all sides. My heart ached as I watched D. A. deal with multiple cases of church discipline for erring believers. Every now and then anger would consume me when I saw my husband mistreated by those he and the other elders had poured their lives into. When numerous people tried to attack my husband's character, my heart fatigued even more. And as a couple we faced one tidal wave after another—family turmoil between us and both sets of parents, our daughter Lola suffering from night terrors, and our family moving four times.

This season of hardship was made even more difficult because D. A. wouldn't open up to me about the tension in his soul. He was trying to protect me by not sharing details of counseling sessions and meetings, and I did learn to appreciate how he was shepherding my heart. However, he would completely shut down when it came to his personal grief and how he was doing emotionally, mentally, and spiritually. As a result, I felt as though I were alone during this time of suffering.

Communication barriers only make seasons of suffering harder. As spouses, we need to be able to connect with each other in these vulnerable times. We're strongest when we're together.

One night when we were lying in bed, D. A. confessed that he couldn't sleep without sharing where his heart was. He began to talk about all the pain he was enduring—his grief over those in the church who were choosing habitual sin over holiness, the tension between us and our parents, his lack of control over Lola's night terrors. He told me that on many nights, he would weep and ask God to prevent him from waking up the next morning. My heart flooded with fear and grief when I heard him say this! I had known he was suffering, but because he had guarded his heart, I had no way of knowing the depth of his grief.

That night we took the conversation to level one, sought the Scriptures, and prayed together. Before going to sleep, we decided to develop an action plan the next morning—a way to face the suffering *together*. We said we would expand our times in prayer to include our griefs and the situations we were facing. We would trust God to lead us.

When people refuse to open up about what they're going through, they're prone to believe they're alone and no one cares for them. Most often, others *do* care—but in the midst of suffering, people are afraid to be vulnerable and share the struggles they're going through. In marriage, this should not be. If there's anyone in addition to God you should open up to, that person has to be your spouse.

Seasons of suffering seem to highlight the rich or poor condition of a marriage. If you're enduring suffering now and you or your spouse have shut down the lines of communication, work together, perhaps even with a third party (such as a marriage counselor or pastor), to rebuild the connection. If you do, you'll both realize you're not suffering in isolation.

Seeking Scripture Together

D. A.

When Elicia and I were working to reopen our lines of communication, we didn't know how to address everything I was struggling with. We agreed to take our burdens before the Lord in prayer and to open up Scripture to receive clarity, correction, and comfort. Only in seeking our Father during this season of suffering would we be able to connect more deeply to each other.

Our journey began in a passage we were both familiar with: Ephesians 6:10-17. After diving deeper into these verses, we discovered the need for, and the function of, the full armor of God, particularly in the battle for a gospel-saturated marriage. Spiritual warfare is a reality in marriage. The last thing Satan wants is for marriages to thrive—couples showing the gospel to everyone around them.

In Ephesians 6:10 the apostle Paul appeals for Christians to "be strong in the Lord and in the strength of his might." He then commands us to "put on the whole armor of God, that [we] may be able to stand against the schemes of the devil" (verse 11). So what are the schemes of the devil in our marriages? How does Satan attack the body of Christ?

The book of Job gives us insight into how limited Satan's power is—he can do only what God allows—because God is sovereign and is in control of all things (Ephesians 1:11). In the season of suffering that Job and his wife went through, they faced pain and tension. Job 2:9-10 actually records a spat between the two. Job's wife felt that God was not treating Job fairly, and in her mind, the reasonable response was for Job to curse God and die. Job snapped back, informing his wife that she was speaking like a nonbeliever. Afterward,

Job renewed his submission to God. In that moment of challenge with his wife, Job did not sin.

It's hard to imitate Job when we're suffering. I'll be the first to admit that my natural responses don't always align with Job's. We are all born with a sinful nature (Ephesians 2:1-3) that is prone to fall into temptation. Satan desires to fill our hearts and minds with doubts regarding God and His Word, a tactic first displayed in the Garden of Eden (Genesis 3:1-7). We fight the enemy by resisting the things he puts before us (1 Peter 5:8-9).

The battle every Christian is fighting is not physical but spiritual. As Paul says in Ephesians 6:12, "We do not wrestle against flesh and blood, but against the rulers, against the authorities, against the cosmic powers over this present darkness, against the spiritual forces of evil in the heavenly places." *People* are not the enemy—rather, it is the spirits who influence and govern the decision processes of people who are not in Christ. And so, in times of spiritual warfare, we must ask God to frequently remind us that our spouses are not the enemy. In Ephesians 2:1-3, Paul speaks of the worldly system in which we live, governed by the "sons of disobedience" and under the dominance of the evil one— the "prince of the power of the air," Satan. As we face these enemies, our spouses are our allies. If we're fighting with each other, we're not fighting the enemy of our souls.

In addition, fighting a spiritual battle with physical weapons will not bring victory. We will triumph only when we put on and utilize the full armor of God (see Ephesians 6:10-18).

God has given this armor to every Christian, but we must make the conscious decision to put it on piece by piece. Each piece of armor has profound implications for how we fight spiritual warfare both individually and together in marriage:

> *"Belt of truth."* We must be truthful in our speech, analyzing our hearts in light of Scripture. When we live out Ephesians 4:21, 24-25, and 5:8-10, we are actively fighting against the temptation to lie, which places our hearts in direct opposition to God's truthful character. In marriage, we put on the belt of truth when we speak honestly with our spouses and read God's Word together so we both can be reminded of His truth.

> *"Breastplate of righteousness."* We must guard our hearts, which means preserving our spiritual integrity. Because our hearts are wicked (Jeremiah 17:9), we must surrender to the Lord to avoid unrighteous words. Our hearts can become prone to doubting God when troubled (or engaged in spiritual warfare), so we must take Jesus' advice in John 14:1: "Believe in God; believe also in me." Spending time in prayer together will help us assess if we and our spouses are wearing the breastplate of righteousness. As we confess our anxieties, fears, and frustrations before the Lord and each other, our motives—the things we have hidden in our hearts—will become exposed, and our spouses will know us more intimately, bathe us in grace, and all the while spur us on

to endure alongside them during the season of suffering or testing. As we confess before God together, we can put on the breastplate and rejoice that God has extended us grace to wear it.

"Shoes; the gospel of peace." We must walk in step with the gospel. The gospel provides Christians both peace *with* God and the peace *of* God. Peace with God was secured through the finished work of Jesus Christ. When we embraced Christ as Savior, we were justified, no longer His enemies, and for eternity we have peace with Him (Romans 5:1). Now, being in Christ (Colossians 3:3), we also can walk through life in the peace of God, no matter what calamity and chaos the enemy throws our way (Psalm 29:11; 85:8; John 14:27; 16:33; Galatians 5:22; Philippians 4:7; Colossians 3:15; 2 Thessalonians 3:16; 1 Peter 5:7). Every step we take should remind us we have both peace with God and the peace of God. Nothing can take that from us. This truth should encourage us to trust in God's leadership during seasons of suffering. If our next steps glorify God and help advance the gospel, we're likely walking in harmony with the Lord's will for our marriages and families.

"Shield of faith." We must put our faith in God and trust in and apply all He has revealed in Scripture (2 Timothy 3:16-17). This shield protects us from the enemy's fiery attacks, specifically the thoughts he strives to plant in our minds. We are safeguarded from the attacks as we filter

every thought through God's Word, which is our rule of faith and practice (2 Corinthians 10:3-6). As we engage in level one or level two conversations with our spouses, we must lean on the Scriptures as much as possible. In these deep conversations, emotions are high and can easily sway us. If each of us filters our emotions, suspicions, and thoughts through Scripture, we can stand firm, acknowledging as true every idea that aligns with Scripture and rejecting every idea that does not.

"Helmet of salvation." The security of salvation protects our minds and thoughts. Those who have placed their trust in Christ must be assured of salvation; otherwise, the enemy will regularly plant doubts in their minds. The enemy is cunning. Before Elicia and I were born again, he had swayed us to believe we were secure in salvation because we went to church. And after the Lord saved us both, we wrestled with doubts about our salvation for our first ten years in the faith! A Christian who doubts his or her salvation is an easy target for the enemy. During such times we must remind ourselves of the gospel message (Romans 10:9-10), assess our hearts (1 John 2:3-6), and go to God's Word for comfort (5:10-13). In marriage we can encourage each other through reminders of the gospel message and God's track record of salvation and the process of sanctification. Remembering God's great work in each of your lives will revive your hearts with joy and gladness toward the One who saved and is sanctifying you.

"Sword of the Spirit." Paul saves the offensive weapon of the armor for last. We must be grounded in God's Word. Scripture is the sword because of its power and effectiveness (Hebrews 4:12). Scripture is called "the sword of the Spirit" because God Himself breathed out His Word (2 Timothy 3:16). Whenever writers wrote down new revelations from God, God the Holy Spirit kept them from writing anything contrary to truth (2 Peter 1:16-21).

Many believers are not walking in the spiritual victory God desires for us because we're not using the sword of the Spirit during times of spiritual battle. We choose other, non-effective weapons that don't come from God. When times of stress in our marriages seek to hold us hostage, we're tempted to turn to coping mechanisms to get through the day. Perhaps we seek comfort by going out to eat, watching movies, or stuffing our faces with Oreo cookies. I wish Elicia and I could say we always turn to Scripture, prayer, and worship music, but the truth is we don't. Often, these options have been our last. We are not walking in spiritual victory because we're not using the spiritual weapons God has given us! It's as though we're soldiers willfully dropping our machine guns and opting to use BB guns instead. A BB gun may look like a real gun, but if the enemy is armed with a real gun, pulling out a BB gun won't deter them—it will only cause them to shoot faster.

When Paul says in Ephesians 6:17, "The sword of the Spirit . . . is the word of God," the Greek term he uses for *word* is *rhēma*, which refers to words that are spoken. Using the sword of the Spirit can include quoting God's Word during battle!

The perfect example of this is Jesus. In Matthew 4:1-11, we see Satan himself tempting Jesus at the end of a forty-day fast. Each time Satan tempted Jesus, Jesus didn't respond by first blowing off steam as we would. Instead, Jesus spoke God's Word. On each of the three occasions He was tempted, He said, "It is written . . ." and then quoted a verse refuting the temptation. He modeled for all who follow Him what walking in spiritual victory looks like!

As believers, we must live out three truths in response to spiritual warfare. First, each of us must choose to put on the full armor of God and challenge our spouses to do the same. God has provided us with this armor, but it's our responsibility to clothe ourselves with it. We do this by living out the implications of each piece's meaning.

Second, we must not go looking for fights with our enemies or with our spouses. Growing up on the streets we used to say, "Don't start nothin', won't be nothin'," which means you won't get beat up or jumped if you don't initiate the fight. However, just as in the streets, trouble has a way of finding you even when you're not looking for it. You and your spouse know how many times you planned on having a relaxing evening only to find yourselves arguing over something so small you can't remember what it was! Be on guard against these fights—the enemy is trying to distract you.

Third, the full armor of God is not to be worn simply for fashion but for the fight on the front line. If we sincerely love Christ and have faith in him, we must not be naive and assume we won't be brought under spiritual attack (1 Thessalonians 3:4; 2 Timothy 3:12; 1 Peter 4:12-16). We must remain "sober-minded" at all times because our enemy is waiting for us to slip up (1 Peter 5:8). Being sober-minded in marriage means both of you are thinking clearly about God and His Word and have a grounded understanding of how to fight as a team instead of as combatants.

In marriage, when both spouses wear the armor of God and leverage each piece for its intended purpose, the entire household has greater opportunity to walk in spiritual victory rather than in defeat. When we're walking in spiritual victory, we'll not only quote God's Word but also apply it! In times of intense spiritual warfare and suffering, God's Word is the most effective tool for encouragement and hope.

Praying and Fasting Together

Elicia

Another important way to fight through times of trial in marriage is to spend time together in prayer. Early in our marriage, I grew frustrated waiting for D. A. to take the lead and initiate times of prayer together. I'm not exaggerating when I say that the only times we prayed together during those first three years were before we ate a meal, when we faced some type of hardship or crisis, and when we needed a financial breakthrough. We were so spiritually immature in our first three years of marriage that we not only struggled to pray together but also lacked consistency in our individual prayer lives.

By God's grace, we were able to develop a rhythm of oneness in the area of prayer after sitting down and asking each other open-ended questions about our prayerlessness. If you're struggling with routinely getting together to pray, then you may find it helpful to sit down as a couple and assess why your prayer life is coming up short. What do your individual prayer lives look like? What's keeping you from praying together at least three times a week? How will your marriage benefit from praying together regularly? After your discussion, you can both develop a plan to move forward together.

Now, before you think that D. A. and I immediately started having three-hour-long prayer sessions, let me share with you a few realistic things about our prayer life together.

We most often pray together before bed. These prayers are usually two or three specific requests we agree on beforehand. We root this practice in Philippians 4:6: "Do not be anxious about anything, but in everything by prayer and supplication with thanksgiving let your requests be made known to God." Our prayer time lasts between five and ten minutes at most, and again and again we've watched in awe as God has answered our specific requests with *yes, no,* or *wait.*

D. A. and I have also committed to pray together regularly about pressing issues until God opens or closes a door.

When D. A. was asked to come on full-time at the church we planted in Kansas City, we struggled with whether I should still work full-time, go part-time, or step away to become a stay-at-home mom. After the Lord opened the door for D. A.'s job, we sensed that I should still work full-time to provide our family with an additional salary and, most importantly, health insurance.

Over the next eighteen months, D. A. and I continued to ask God for guidance about my job, and the church was finally able to pay for our family's health coverage. D. A. became an adjunct professor at the Bible college we graduated from, and his itinerant speaking schedule began to bring in a steady flow of income. We both felt that at that point God opened the door for me to step away from my job altogether so that I could begin to homeschool our older daughter, Bella.

Another important component of our prayer life is our shared desire to intercede for other people. Before we go before the Lord together, we share about providential meetings, the needs of family and friends, and text messages with urgent requests. Romans 8:26-27 gives us confidence in intercessory prayer—that even as we're trying to think of what to say, or stumbling through our heartfelt prayer, God the Holy Spirit makes perfect intercession through us! In addition, Jesus Himself intercedes on our behalf (Hebrews 7:25) while God the Father hears our requests and answers our prayers in accordance to His will (1 John 5:14-15).

On a few occasions, when we were burdened by anxiety,

confusion, frustration, and suffering, we mutually agreed to fast. Isaiah 58 simply says the fasting that God desires is a denial of selfishness while offering true worship to God and serving others—being a burden taker rather than a burden maker. Sometimes D. A. and I dedicate a day for fasting from sunup to sundown. We go about our workdays as normal, and when lunchtime comes, we work to get away and spend time with the Lord individually. When we're at home, we make sure the kids eat dinner, and after they go to bed we connect to read Scripture, pray, and close our fast by sharing a small meal or snack. During more difficult times, we've dedicated a full day to fasting at least once or twice a week, sometimes for up to four weeks. Our focus is asking God to reveal our sinfulness, show us areas in which He's calling us to mature, provide wisdom, and remove our selfish desires and replace them with His desires for us.

Praying and fasting together as a married couple will immensely benefit your marriage. And each spouse has freedom in Christ to develop his or her own rhythm in prayer. Some of your prayers may last five minutes, and others may go on for an extended period. Sometimes you may choose to fast from sunup to sundown; other times your fast may go on for a couple of days. As with all your times of praying and fasting, the entire Trinity is involved, so be encouraged to go before the throne of God together as husband and wife. If you both are in Christ, you have access to your Father because of the finished work of Jesus (Hebrews 4:14-16).

Upheld by Community

D. A.

Knowing the spiritual warfare that accompanies church planting, we started praying for our move to Los Angeles in 2014, right after the Lord provided the green light. Within weeks of praying for spiritual strength, Elicia was diagnosed with multiple sclerosis. Her health condition prevented her from homeschooling, and my job transition—a role at the North American Mission Board (NAMB) to continue preparing us for our eventual migration to LA—moved us from Decatur to Cumming, Georgia. The move put us fifty minutes from our church home in downtown Atlanta. Constant drama with family both near and far added to the sense of isolation.

As time went on, we began to run on fumes as a family. Los Angeles was still on our hearts, but we decided we wouldn't allow our weariness to lead us into making a rash decision about moving there. At this point, I had settled into my role at NAMB, but other job offers had emerged: a full-time teaching position at the university level (a dream come true) and a residency program in Raleigh, North Carolina, at Summit Church.

Should we stay where we are or go into one of these new roles? we wondered. None of the options was sinful, but because we were suffering and wrestling with isolation, we knew we had to seek counsel and be of one mind as husband and wife before moving.

Truth be told, we just wanted to be in LA already, but we knew that heading out there with little or no gas left in the tank would crush our entire family. After weeks of constant prayer and some fasting, Elicia and I made the decision to head to Summit Church for ten months to be commissioned by them to plant in Los Angeles.

The move to Raleigh went well, as did our first few months there. For Thanksgiving, we headed to Kansas City to celebrate with all our family before our move out West—we knew trips to see our parents would be few and far between once we got out there.

Just after returning to our apartment in North Carolina—I had brought in our last bag a moment before—Elicia came running to me, asking what happened to my cousin. She had been scrolling through Facebook and saw a post from one of my family members, expressing grief over my cousin's sudden death. I was totally unaware, and my heart erupted with grief.

I walked away from Elicia and went into our bedroom. I was numb. I felt nothing. I heard nothing. I closed my eyes, envisioning my cousin at age fourteen, begging me, age fifteen, to leave the rebellious life in the streets and turn to Jesus. I drifted in thought for a few more minutes and watched the multitudes of interactions between her and me whisk by. When I opened my eyes, Elicia was standing in front of me. Immediately I reached out to hug her, and as soon as we embraced, I wept uncontrollably.

My daughters walked into our room with disbelief. The *machismo*[1] inside of me didn't want them to see me like this, but I needed them to. I needed my wife to hold me up as I fell limp in her arms. Seasons of suffering are hard on both spouses, but some seasons strike one person harder than the other. We need to be ready to hold up our spouses—and we need to be ready to grieve and let our spouses hold us. This is what oneness looks like in marriage. In this particular season, God used Elicia to hold me up.

Losing my cousin affected both Elicia and me because we both knew her. The following days were tough. I had to travel to West Palm Beach, Florida, for a fund-raising meeting for our church plant. Right before my flight took off, my phone rang. It was Ricky, a close friend of mine back in Kansas City, who was also a member of the church I had pastored. Knowing I had only a few minutes before takeoff, I didn't accept the call but instead texted him to see if he was okay. He texted back to tell me that J. R., his cousin and one of my dearest friends since the age of five, had passed away suddenly of a heart attack. Ricky told me it was not public, but he wanted me to know because of how close J. R. and I were when we were growing up. My plane took off, and I lost cell connection.

To say I was devastated is an understatement. First my cousin and then J. R. When I landed, I texted Elicia and told her J. R. was gone. She, too, was in shock.

Numbness held my body hostage. As people were rushing past me to make their connecting flights, I sat there with no strength to rise. I cried out to God for hope in this despair and asked Him for grace as I was about to interview with a ministry that was considering investing in our church plant in LA. I was scheduled to meet with these investors at a restaurant in the airport, but first I made a beeline to the men's restroom to wash the tearstains from my face. When I gained my composure, I walked to the restaurant and met Dr. Joe and Liana Guethon and their son. Their smiling faces brought my soul comfort.

I wear my life on my face, and as soon as they saw me, they asked if I was okay. I couldn't lie—I told them of J. R.'s passing and how it had occurred just days after my cousin's. They offered me not only condolences but also heartfelt prayers and timely words of biblical counsel and hope. That time was healing salve to my bleeding heart. Our fellowship was so sweet that I almost missed my flight back to North Carolina!

When I got home, I poured out my heart to Elicia, and we wept together. J. R. was buried right after Christmas, and I wasn't able to attend. While I was dealing with the grief of not making J. R.'s funeral, my brother Raymond texted me news of another family friend's passing. By this time, Elicia and I were left wondering, *What's next, God?* Little did we know that the next wave would hit us even closer to home.

When our son, Duce, was born, we were told that he needed to have the skin under his tongue clipped. The doctors said we could expect some delay in speech and possible impediments, but that overall, with some assistance, he would be okay. After he turned two years old, he started screaming . . . almost nonstop. It got so bad at night that we were scared he would wake up our neighbors. Duce wasn't using many words; instead he would scream, grow frustrated, and hit himself. We felt so helpless, and our hearts were breaking because we didn't know what he was trying to communicate.

Elicia decided to follow the doctor's referral for an assessment, and on the day of the appointment, Duce woke up screaming at 5:45 a.m. (possible night terrors). Elicia and I tried to console him, but he didn't go back to sleep, and neither did we. By 7:30 a.m. we had to wake up the girls for school and start our day. I headed to the office and asked Elicia to keep me in the loop regarding his appointment, which was set for 2:00 p.m.

On my way home, I called Elicia as she was driving Duce to his appointment. She said that he'd just fallen asleep, which was not good. Elicia was almost at the doctor's office, meaning Duce's nap would be only about twenty minutes long—worse than him not taking a nap at all.

My daughters and I ate lunch, and then I took them to our neighborhood park for the afternoon. It was getting dark, and I hadn't heard from Elicia, so I texted her at six and asked if she was okay. Fifteen minutes later she called me, crying hysterically. I couldn't make out what she was saying until she suddenly screamed, "They think he has autism!"

Everything came to a screeching halt. Grief once again consumed both Elicia and me. For the remainder of the night, we wrestled with the what-ifs and didn't sleep much.

The next day I reached out to some of the pastors at Summit for counsel. Duce's potential diagnosis of autism was the straw breaking the camel's back—I was not ready to plant a church. I committed to Elicia that I'd do anything for the health of our family—I was willing to walk away from the plant in LA if our son's diagnosis was confirmed. This, along with Elicia's multiple sclerosis diagnosis, was just too much.

In God's grace, we received counsel to get a second opinion, and everything checked out okay with Duce. We placed a heavier emphasis on his speech exercises, and we were so fortunate that the Lord blessed us by calling our friend Whitney, a member of Summit Church and an expert in child speech pathology, to join our church plant.

Whitney has been with us every step of the way and provides us with constant insights and wisdom on how to work with our son and his speech development. God used our family at Summit Church, whom we had known for only a few months, to come alongside us while we were facing various afflictions. This community loved us well during this particular season of suffering.

Looking back over almost fifteen years of marriage, whenever our times of suffering seemed to be getting worse, God the Holy Spirit provided us with opportunities to drop our pride and come together. We are fully convinced that a gospel-saturated marriage opens up lines of transparent communication not only between spouses but also with other believers we are living in fellowship with.

Seasons of suffering tempt us to run into isolation, but God has wired us to live in community, reflecting His Trinitarian nature. Therefore a gospel-saturated marriage needs a healthy commitment to a local church. The body of Christ is made up of the souls Jesus has saved (1 Peter 2:5), who are interdependently connected and designed to work together (1 Corinthians 12:12-27).

The Lord will equip you and your spouse to endure seasons of suffering for your good and for His glory (Romans 8:28), and the body of Christ will be there to both rejoice and weep with you (Romans 12:15). And sometimes you and your spouse will hear of brothers and sisters in your local body who need you, and together you will be able to comfort them during their time of affliction (2 Corinthians 1:3-7).

The world wants to see your seasons of suffering break your marriage apart, but God has designed suffering to strengthen your marriage. When times get overwhelming, seek Scripture, pray, and fast together. Pursue the saints in your local church, and watch God turn tragedy into triumph. And then rejoice—"The sufferings of this present time are not worth comparing with the glory that is to be revealed to us" (Romans 8:18).

As God supplies you and your spouse with endurance, be comforted: through Christ, your marriage can and will go the distance!

CHAPTER 5

IT STARTS AT HOME

If it is evil in your eyes to serve the LORD, choose this day whom
you will serve, whether the gods your fathers served in the region
beyond the River, or the gods of the Amorites in whose land you
dwell. But as for me and my house, we will serve the LORD.

JOSHUA 24:15

D. A.

In cultures around the world, the family is the basic unit of society.[1] Christians in America should recognize this as well. The interpersonal relationships inside our homes are the most crucial. This includes not only the marital relationship but also the relationship with our children.

Every personal narrative is different, and every family structure looks different. Some Christian homes consist of a husband and wife with their biological children. Others are made up of one believing and one nonbelieving spouse, blended families, single parents, grandparents or other guardians raising children, or families with foster and adopted children. Each of these homes is equally precious in the eyes of God. There are no second-class citizens in God's Kingdom.

With that said, this chapter is focused on setting a goal for all believers to live out their roles in gospel-saturated homes. Families who love Jesus and are daily living out the implications of their faith in Christ are desperately needed in our cities and nation. We pray that more Christian families become healthy systems of discipleship, walking in authentic love toward one another. As families do this, our homes will become places where God's love flows out in action to our neighbors and communities. It's crucial that a husband and wife work together to discern and understand God's call for their entire family, and they must be wise and intentional about how they approach discipleship.

In this chapter, we want to focus on the spiritual climate of Christian homes. We will look at the biblical roles of husbands, wives, and children—specifically how each relationship should be a form of discipleship. If nonbelievers are part of the family dynamic, our relationships need to be evangelistic, and our discipleship rhythms among believers should be a compelling witness to the nonbelievers.

We define *discipleship* as a maturing believer taking an immature believer by the hand and walking together for a season, which is the model seen in 2 Timothy 2:2. A time will come when both are more mature in Christ than when they started, and they are then peers equally engaged in the work of discipleship, seeking less mature believers to lead into maturity. This process should be repeated until each believer sees the Lord face-to-face.

Discipleship First

Discipleship between spouses is the foundation for a discipleship culture in the home. As we disciple each other, we help each other grow in living out our assigned biblical roles. Both spouses should feel the freedom to contribute to the discipleship relationship. For example, sometimes I will read and unpack the Scriptures to Elicia, and she will respond with insights, introduce parallel passages, and call both of us to apply the principles in our marriage. We both take time to pray and confess our fears, frustrations, and sins, and we correct each other in love as we work through the pressures and trials of church, home, and work. Our rhythm of discipleship waters the seeds we sow into the lives of our children, others we're in discipleship relationships with, and friends in various seasons of life.

Trust us—this is not easy. Discipleship is intrusive, messy, unattractive, and hard work. Yet so is marriage. A discipleship relationship between saved spouses should be automatic, but since we all still wrestle with our flesh, it can be achieved only through high levels of intentionality and sacrifice.

Because spouses may enter marriage at different levels of spiritual maturity, each spouse should strive to put a personal holistic discipleship team in place before getting married. This team should consist of at least three types of people who are presently engaged in discipleship with the individual: a

Parent (someone who is more seasoned in the faith), a Peer (a peer in the faith), and a Pupil (someone whom the spouse is discipling). These people will provide a holistic view of accountability.

A Parent can correct, guide, and speak biblical truth into our lives, especially in times of confusion. A Peer is in a similar season of life (newlywed or engaged) and can spur us on to holy living. A Pupil asks questions that cause us to reflect and teach the biblical and contextualized content we've gleaned from the Parent and Peer.

If you're married and do not have these kinds of people in your life, don't fret—it's never too late. First, pray and ask the Lord to open the doors for such relationships. According to Ephesians 4:11-16, Christ Jesus won't leave you hanging when it comes to relationships that lead you in spiritual maturity! Second, begin to seek relationships with people of the same gender in each of the three categories listed. This is where the local church comes in. It would be wise to seek meaningful relationships while helping your spouse do the same.

Sometimes these people, especially the Parents in your life, may be in different geographic locations because God connected you to them in a previous season of life. Such relationships are not bound by geography; however, strive to find relationships nearby as well. It's less likely for someone in your local church to be fooled when you try to paint yourself in a better light. A nearby Parent can add up context clues from your life's rhythm, online posts, and facial expressions and will blow the whistle on you when he or she sees inaccuracies in your story. Someone not living near you may not know such things unless you tell them.

First John 2:12-14 provides a biblical rationale for such relationships. Here we see John identify three types of Christians: "little children" (Pupils), "fathers" (Parents), and "young men" (Peers). People functioning in each of these three roles will help us love God and our spouses more and not love the world (1 John 2:15-17).

When these relationships are in place, your spouse knows that even if you're not listening to each other, you have at least three other voices of reasonable counsel who are challenging you from God's Word to remain faithful in your mutual discipleship relationship.

And what exactly does a discipleship relationship in marriage look like? The ingredients should include reading Scripture together, listening to sermons and discussing their application in the home, praying together, fasting in dedicated and defined times together, and taking retreats to strengthen togetherness.

Here are some ways we apply these ingredients in our own marriage:

Reading Scripture. We select a book of the Bible and work through it individually, then come together to discuss.

Listening to sermons. We listen to sermons from trusted pastors and discuss.

Praying together. We share our anxieties, fears, and frustrations and then pray through them together.

Fasting. We decide on what we're fasting from, set a time line (e.g., twenty-four hours, two days), and engage in prayer (individually and together) regarding our closeness to God and each other.

Taking retreats. Sometimes this involves weekend getaways, but because life doesn't always allow the money or time, we set the bedtime for our kids at eight or eight thirty. This gives us at least two hours of uninterrupted alone time—to do things such as watch Netflix, review our family calendar, discuss issues of the heart, be intimate, or eat sweets without the kids asking us to share.

When we hit a wall in our relationship and can't agree on an issue, each of us goes to speak with those we're in discipleship relationships with. We speak candidly about the issue we're facing and ask them to uncover our blind spots and counsel us—to humble our hearts so a mutual decision can be made. These people keep Elicia and me from butting heads over small things and help us have the energy and ability to disciple each other. It's a blessing to walk with friends in the body of Christ who can challenge us to humble ourselves before each other, admit when we are wrong, forgive, and move forward in unity.

In marriage, we must be ready to lovingly challenge each

other. Elicia and I are deeply in love and are very transparent in our relationship; however, transparency doesn't always equal full truthfulness. There have been times we've purposefully withheld information from each other out of embarrassment. Other times we've outright lied to save face and have broken trust over the smallest of issues, shedding many tears of repentance. In God's grace, we love each other enough to confront the other person's lie, continue to trust each other, remain open, and humble our hearts by welcoming correction at any moment.

As believers, we see the transformative work of God the Holy Spirit when we couple transparency with complete truthfulness. These attributes allow us to teach and spur one another on "to love and good works" (Hebrews 10:24). Once we establish our discipleship relationships, we will begin to walk more closely in line with God's design for manhood and womanhood.

Husbands

Ephesians 5:25-32 is a helpful passage when it comes to discussing biblical roles for husbands and wives. These verses provide three clear practical applications that husbands should strive to live out. Biblical husbands are called to (1) sacrifice purposefully, (2) seek to purify, and (3) steadily provide. As a high calling, husbands are called to emulate Jesus Christ Himself, having been given the privilege of loving their wives as Jesus loves His bride, the church.

Sacrifice Purposefully

Through the order of creation that we see in Genesis, God has established the husband as the leading authority figure in the home. Now, I need to be very clear about what this means: The husband is not an authoritarian; rather, his authority should be set within mutual submission, as described in Ephesians 5:21. When we who are believers live under the influence of God the Holy Spirit (Ephesians 5:18-21), we will not seek to force our desires on others, especially our spouses. Spirit-filled living will allow us to find a gospel-saturated balance, leading our home while not abusing our position.

As husbands, we are called to follow the example of Jesus, who gave up His full rights, namely the full expression of His deity, to fulfill His responsibility to love the church. This love meant giving His life for her! To live according to this model, we must strive for the kind of humility we see in Philippians 2:1-10, where Jesus, who is fully God, humbles Himself before God the Father. In fact, Paul says Jesus humbled Himself by taking on the form of a servant. In the same way, we—as biblical husbands—must strive to lead our families chiefly by serving them.

The reward for this life of purposeful sacrifice is the daily privilege of joining our wives in sanctification. We must make sure that how we treat our wives every day helps, not hinders, their walk with Christ. This is a challenge! I encourage you to sit down with your wife and ask her the following questions so you can gauge where you are excelling and where you can improve:

Communication. "Do the tone of my voice and my non-verbal body language upset you regularly, or do they typically reassure you? How can I improve these aspects of my communication?"

Listening. "Do you feel that I pay attention to you daily? In what ways do you feel I'm not listening well?"

Time Together. "Do I make time for you and keep you as a priority, or do you feel as though I put you on the back burner? What things do I do that cause you to feel either way?"

Your wife's answers will reveal how you help or hinder her sanctification. This is crucial—how you treat your wife will determine if you are an encouragement in her growing relationship with God or a barrier and distraction. When I have asked Elicia these types of questions, her answers have humbled me. Sometimes she's told me my tone was cold and harsh. And she's expressed her frustration and hurt when I haven't listened to her and when I haven't carved out space for time alone with her.

Yet the more I work on loving her as Christ loves the church—hearing her heart and actively engaging with what she shares—the more she vocalizes her joy in seeing me love her the way she desires to be loved. I realized that when I asked her a question but then cut her off because I didn't agree with her answer, I frustrated the process, and she would leave the conversation feeling hurt.

If you ask your wife these questions and get negative feedback, don't let that deter you from loving her like Christ would. Keep on putting in the work to love her. God will do a great work in both of your hearts, causing her to trust you in your God-given role to help her become more pure before God.

Seek to Purify

Jesus loves the church through action, cleansing and purifying her through the washing of His Word. As biblical husbands, we should strive to imitate this work of Christ. We are called to speak about Scripture with our wives on a consistent basis and challenge them to apply passages in their lives— allowing them the same space to challenge us as well.

However, any time we speak hard or challenging things into the life of our spouse, we need to think of our words in terms of a bank account. Before we can make a withdrawal, we have to make a deposit—and the amount deposited should always exceed the amount withdrawn. If we attempt to use more than what is in the account, there will be consequences for our actions.

In real life, we'll face overdraft fees or a declined card, but in marriage the stakes are much higher. We must make deposits that equate to words of affirmation and time in the Scriptures together before we make withdrawals (words of challenge or correction). When our wives see us regularly making deposits, they will be more likely to readily accept timely counsel from us regarding life transformation.

For years I was fearful of calling out Elicia's sin because I dreaded her response, even though she had asked me to do this. I knew we'd end up arguing, bringing up past issues, and it would ultimately create an uneasy tension in our home. I realized that when we weren't spending much time in Scripture together, due to my lack in leading us in Bible study, she was even more resistant to telling me about things she had done that might offend me. But regularly reading Scripture and praying together didn't guarantee success either—challenging each other in private about specific issues of sin often resulted in one of us responding in the flesh.

Despite my fears, however, my love for my wife and her purity before God, our children, and the world became more of a priority to me than worrying about her reactions. I learned to approach her in a few key ways: I would be as objective with truth as possible, assessing her actions in light of Scripture; I would offer an example of how I had fallen into a similar lapse of judgment, identifying with the embarrassment, guilt, and frustration she felt; and I would walk with my wife to the cross and embrace forgiveness in Christ alongside her. At the same time, Elicia has held me accountable, called out my sinfulness, and allowed space for me to openly confess and repent.

This process allows us to recognize the gospel as our hope especially when we fail. The gospel produces community, and walking in repentance has a higher success rate when it's done together. In our marriage, we both desire to grow to maturity in Christ. Maturity cannot happen without correction, and gospel-saturated correction leads us to such maturity.

Steadily Provide

As biblical husbands, we should ask God for the conviction to serve our spouses (and children) by feeding and nourishing them. We feed and nourish our families when we (1) lead them to God's Word and model for them what it looks like to try to be a doer of what we read (James 1:22-25) and (2) provide space for them to be doers of God's Word.

One way I've worked to do this in my marriage is by providing Elicia with space to have personal time with God, as well as discipleship and evangelistic time and fellowship with other women. I was challenged to do this while serving as a pastor in Kansas City. One day Elicia asked me if I would be okay with her inviting women over on Tuesday mornings for discipleship time.

I was ecstatic. Elicia had always shown me grace when I wanted to meet with men from the church—how could I deny her the same? For the next couple of years, most Tuesday mornings from five thirty to eight, our house was filled with as many as twelve women who were striving to mature in Christ. Now that we're living in Long Beach, Elicia hosts other women so they can develop meaningful friendships.

Elicia has shared her heart with me and helps me know how I can serve her while she's serving others. It's my joy to help wake up the kids, feed them breakfast, and get their school day started so that Elicia can engage in meaningful dialogue with these ladies.

Watching Elicia excel in discipleship and hospitality has drawn my heart to cherish her more. As I read Ephesians 5:29, I'm seeing with greater clarity what Paul meant when he charged husbands to nourish (feed) and cherish (take care of) their wives. He's asking men to regularly show their wives loving affection in addition to providing comfort, contentment, and security.

Women differ in their emotional, financial, physical, and spiritual needs, which is why healthy communication between spouses is necessary. It is of no value to my marriage if I provide for Elicia only in generic ways, all the while neglecting her specific needs. Elicia is the one I've covenanted with; her needs are my priority, and she alone should tell me what those needs are. Through consistent conversation and with patience for both of us, I should not only strive to show her affection but also check in with her often to make sure she's feeling secure.

Sometimes I can offer her security not by what I provide but by telling her I don't have the answer and that we need to seek God together. There was a time when I was unemployed for a few months and another time when our health insurance premiums went from $700 a month to $2,100 a month, and I didn't know what we were going to do. The only hope I could give Elicia was reminding her I was limited in my power—I could keep making phone calls and putting in applications, but that was the most I could do. However, together we could beg God to intervene.

Each time we'd get hit with such issues, God always pulled through. Elicia saw that Jesus was the true provider for our family, and I was able to help her steward what He blessed us with.

I will be the first to tell you that I fail at being a biblical husband every single day—yet, in God's grace and with much patience from my wife, I desire to improve with each passing day.

Sometimes, though, I fall short of following Peter's instructions to be understanding toward my wife (1 Peter 3:7) or to share my inward struggles with her. Being understanding toward my wife means listening to her and letting her know I'm hearing her heart. The Lord challenges me daily to study Elicia so that I will be able to discern when it's appropriate to joke and when it's time to put away all distractions so she feels safe to share her heart.

We gain understanding when we practice knowledge and wisdom. Knowledge comes from content, and if I'm not allowing my wife time to share with me the content of her heart, I'll never really get to know her. Wisdom is the application of knowledge. After my wife shares her heart, giving me knowledge of her hurt, joy, or struggles, I can be active in letting her know I want to walk with her through the issues she's facing. By doing this, I'll gain understanding.

As Christian husbands, we should make it our primary goal to present our wives before God as spotless brides. We'll be more tuned in to doing this as we seek to understand them more. We must also recognize that the discipleship relationship between us and our wives is stifled when we don't work to understand their hearts or share with them the depth of our hearts. We must learn to find a balance so each spouse can remain on the same page. Discipleship can only thrive when both partners walk through life at the same pace, side-by-side.

Wives

Elicia

Okay, now that we have some context about what a biblical husband looks like, let's talk about being a biblical wife. To really understand what it means to be a biblical wife, we have to start with a concept that comes with a lot of baggage. Yup, you know the one I'm talking about: *submission*. Because this word can have negative connotations, I want to explain how I'm defining it.

In a marriage relationship, a wife's submission should not be seen as slavery (Ephesians 5:22-24); rather, submission emerges out of respect for God's order of creation (1 Corinthians 11:12). Submission involves us entrusting ourselves to God (1 Peter 2:23), living with respectful behavior toward our husbands (1 Peter 3:1-2), developing godly character (1 Peter 3:3-5), choosing to do what's right (1 Peter 3:6), and not participating in activities that are sinful and contrary to Scripture. Based on this definition, a biblical wife should find no issue with living in submission to her husband.

Proverbs 31:10-31 exemplifies what it looks like to operate within the framework of freedom that comes with biblical submission. In this passage we see three characteristics of the biblical wife: She is precious, she is productive, and she is praised. She does not boast about herself—rather, her husband, her children, and others declare her to be a woman of high caliber.

She Is Priceless

A biblical wife is a rare and precious thing. Verse 10 says, "She is far more precious than jewels." The writer of this proverb is highlighting the rarity of such a woman. Basically, if a man is blessed to find a biblical wife, he needs to never let her go, no matter what the world offers. The value of the biblical wife is found not in her physical appearance, length of hair, educational credentials, or ability to cook, but rather in her character and how she lives.

Character, like precious metals, is proven through the fiery trials of life. James 1:2-5 says, "Count it all joy, my brothers, when you meet trials of various kinds, for you know that the testing of your faith produces steadfastness. And let steadfastness have its full effect, that you may be perfect and complete, lacking in nothing. If any of you lacks wisdom, let him ask God, who gives generously to all without reproach, and it will be given him." It's hard to think about finding joy when being hit with trials from all sides; however, our joy comes because those trials are purging us of our impurities.

The language Paul uses for *testing* points us toward the

process of goldsmiths or silversmiths who put their elements into the fire to burn away impurities. Once they are gone, the purified metal is soft and ready to be shaped into whatever form the smith desires.

This is a timely illustration for us as biblical wives. As we encounter various levels of relational drama, stress from work (and kids—or both), and other emotional struggles, we are actually being given the opportunity for our character to be proven true! Before we enter the process, many impurities are present in our hearts. But when we are in the fire, as we seek the Lord for strength and grace, they melt away. When this happens, we're ready to be used by God for His glory—He's given us the wisdom we cried out for!

She Is Productive

A biblical wife is productive in ways that complement her husband. Productive means "yielding results, benefits, or profits,"[2] and thus our productivity—our ability to use what we've been given toward good results—extends to many areas of life, such as career, emotions, finances, friendships, hobbies, and parenting.

As an example, let's work through Proverbs 31:11. In this verse, the author says that the husband of a biblical wife has confidence in the way she handles money. He does not walk in the fear that she will spend it all and bring the family to ruin.

In our marriage, I handle the bulk of the finances. This is for our benefit. I'm not throwing D. A. under the bus—he admits this in public all the time. He and I have two different economic philosophies. D. A. says, "Work hard, play hard," so when he takes us out, he spares no expense. When our kids ask him for something, he buys name brand and top of the line. It's sweet that he wants to spoil us, and it's okay because he doesn't do it all the time. Growing up, he didn't have much—his brother Raymond provided for him when his parents couldn't—and he wants to give our kids things he never had.

Me? I'm what D. A. calls the coupon queen! I will shop for clothes out of season (to get better deals); travel to three different grocery stores to buy the best quality groceries for the right price; and save, save, save money rather than spend it. We truly are on opposite ends of the spectrum when it comes to finances! However, we make it work because D. A. trusts me with balancing our accounts, paying bills, and saving money. At the same time, when he wants to splurge on something, he'll come to me (sometimes with a full PDF proposal in hand—no joke) and talk through what he wants to buy. Building this type of trust took time, but it has kept us from staying up late arguing over money like we used to do early in our marriage.

A biblical wife also exhibits productivity through her work ethic. Verses 13, 18, and 24 indicate the wife in this proverb was an entrepreneur—she carefully selected materials, purchased them, and created products that made her family money. Now, ladies, don't think you have to start a business to be a biblical wife! Not every wife will have this kind of opportunity.

But every biblical wife is called to be diligent with what she's been given. When we read verses 16-19, we see the biblical wife burning the midnight oil to make sure her tasks are complete. We all must work hard wherever we're called to do so—whether in a career, at home, or both—and we must identify the things that distract us from getting tasks done.

Sometimes, the amount of time I spend on social media has been a distraction. Other times I've been distracted by the drama that comes with raising three kids, one of whom is a teenager. But I still have work deadlines to meet, friendships to cultivate, and household tasks to complete. Balancing all these things challenges me to a strong work ethic. A strong work ethic glorifies God. And when our families recognize our consistent work ethic, they will likely eagerly support us and our ideas.

For example, I like to let off steam through home interior design projects. D. A. has always supported me in this passion. The first time we walked into our new home in the Long Beach area, I had visions for how I wanted to decorate it, particularly through creating artistic decor that could act as gospel conversation starters. Within the first year of living in our new home, I was able to complete more than a dozen projects, including a full coffee bar for D. A., a wall piece imaging God's call on our family to plant a church, and a grace-themed buffet. I viewed each design project as a reward for being a good steward of my time and family resources. Each one, for me, shows God's fingerprints on our family's home and life rhythm. And every biblical wife has this same freedom to flourish in her passions as she stewards what God has provided for her and her family, and in ways that honor and glorify Him.

Productivity also extends to a wife's attitude toward serving others. For example, verse 15 speaks of how this biblical wife arose early to care for her family and servants. Now, we must again understand that these things are not going to be the norm for every household. We are not disqualified as biblical wives if we don't have servants or get up early in the morning to take care of everyone! But the heart of the biblical wife is what's important. She had a heart of selflessness, and this is what we're called to embrace. This woman had servants, but she took the time to serve not only her children but also those she hired to help. She did what wasn't required of her simply to bless others! May each of us share this heart.

Verse 20 clues us in to the fact that a biblical wife regularly gives to those who are in need, using her resources to benefit others. Financial generosity is one way to help those in need; however, perhaps the greatest resource every woman has equally is time. God has given each of us twenty-four hours in a day, and what we do with them shows where our hearts are.

We can meet the needs of others with our time. Perhaps it's inviting a stressed-out mother and her kids over for a playdate while the two of you take time to talk, open up the Bible, and pray. Maybe it's volunteering to watch a couple's kids so the husband and wife can go on their first date night in ages. Perhaps it's taking a meal to a family who is sick or celebrating the birth of a new child. A biblical wife hears of a need and seeks to meet it, and if she personally can't, she networks with other women or families to help meet the need.

Biblical wives are also productive in how they care for the practical needs of their families. In verse 21, we see that they help prepare their families for the seasonal changes in life. I do this with what D. A. jokingly calls my "thousands" of plastic totes. Of course we don't have thousands, but we do have a lot. They're good for storing things and are easy to move when we relocate! Twice a year I gather the family to prepare for the spring/summer and fall/winter seasons. Everyone knows that on one Saturday before the season hits, we will pack our current clothes in totes and then go to the garage and get our totes for the upcoming season, wash the clothes, and place them in our closets. This is how I prepare my family for seasonal changes and ensure they have the appropriate clothing for the weather. This is a practice I have instilled in my daughters and one I hope they will continue when they're in their own homes.

Verses 22-24 show how a biblical wife's productivity allows her and her family to enjoy the benefits of her stewardship. She has the ability to dress well (after she's taken care of others), and because of her excellent work ethic, others speak well of her husband. This is the picture of togetherness God desires couples to have as they complement each other by living to fulfill God's mission for their family together. A biblical wife understands that carving out time for herself and doing things that bring her joy is not sinful, because her track record of diligent stewardship provides reason for it.

In verses 25-27, we see that the biblical wife "does not eat the bread of idleness" by doing nothing while demanding that her husband do everything. She eats because she put in the work that enables her to do so. Her husband does not find her hard work and productivity threatening—in fact, Lord willing, he celebrates it! Gospel saturation brings harmony between husbands and wives. The biblical husband will empower and champion his wife, encouraging her to leverage productivity in her areas of giftedness. As the wife does this, she brings glory to God and imparts grace to her family.

She Is Praised

Being praised for our role as biblical wives should not be our goal, but we see from Proverbs that this kind of wife is indeed praised and honored by those around her because of who she is and what she does. Verse 28 says that her children and husband praise her for all the great things she does regularly behind closed doors. Ladies, this is our best testimony! It's not about how many followers we have on social media or how in demand we are to speak or teach. Those things do not measure our character because people only see us at our best when we're posting online or speaking publicly. But if we are biblical wives, our families know we care for them and love them no matter who is watching.

Many women in the world possess charm and beauty, but a biblical wife's character sets her apart from all other women (verses 30-31). Charm is limited; it can easily be a facade women hide behind, and it fades as we become more known and our filters fade away. The same can be said of beauty—it's like a vapor, here today and gone tomorrow. As biblical wives, we should accept any praise we receive as a reflection of our fear of the Lord, not as a reflection of our personality (charm) or looks (beauty). The praise we receive from others should point back to our right relationship with God!

Many times I have failed to live up to these expectations. I don't always respond to my husband and children in a way that is pleasing and honoring to God. Yet my hope rests not in my performance but in Christ Jesus. His perfect life fulfilled all of God's requirements for me. When I embraced Jesus as my Savior, God covered me with His righteousness, not my own righteousness. The truth of the gospel encourages me to keep striving to be a biblical wife even when I fail in doing so. And I pray that at the end of my life, any praise will be to God for His work in me and how I fanned the flame for holy living in my husband, children, and other saints' lives in our local church.

Gospel-Saturated Parenting

D. A.

As we talked about before, every family looks different. Every family has a unique and beautiful story that God is still writing. While we can't speak to every family situation in this book, we do want to affirm the importance of biblically informed parenting practices within the gospel-saturated marriage. Over the past years, we've made plenty of mistakes, and we pray our transparency helps you start conversations about gospel-saturated parenting and create encouraging rhythms for your family.

Scripture clearly expresses that children are a blessing (Psalm 127:3-5) and need to be guided rightly by their parents in theological shaping (Deuteronomy 11:19). In addition, children should be disciplined in a way that includes instruction (Proverbs 13:24; 22:15; 23:13-14; 29:15). We see a beautiful picture of parents following God's call to guide their children in 2 Timothy 1, when the apostle Paul talks about the spiritual deposits made in Timothy's life by his mother and grandmother (verse 5). Mothers, never underestimate the power of your biblical investments in the lives of your children! I am a product of one such mother.

Scripture also has clear commands for children. Children are to obey their parents (Exodus 20:12; Ephesians 6:1-3; Colossians 3:20). Paul restates the fifth commandment in the New Testament to emphasize its importance. Obedience to parents, unless the parents are telling their children to sin, is obedience to God. Children who listen to wise instruction from their godly parents will be less likely to fall into the consequences of sinful living.

Elicia and I both failed to listen to the counsel of our parents during our preteen and teenage years and found ourselves in situations that were compromising and dangerous. Only by God's grace were our lives spared on numerous occasions. But even during our rebellious days of running the streets and living in sin, the godly training from our parents and pastors would echo in the back of our minds. Our friends who didn't have regular exposure to God's Word had no such conviction. Some of those friends are now addicted to drugs or doing time in prison—or they've died. Others are wrestling with their demons from decades of addiction, or, by God's grace, crying out to Jesus for salvation after years of living in the fast lane.

Biblical parents must create the spiritual climate of the home. This, however, doesn't mean we can control our children's spiritual trajectories. Perhaps one of the hardest lessons we've had to learn is that God—not Elicia and I—is writing the testimonies of our children. So often we want to control every detail of our children's lives; however, this is simply not possible. What we are to do instead is expose our children to God by sharing the gospel, unpacking the Scriptures, and, most importantly, living out the same biblical convictions we are calling them to live.

According to Pew Research, children who grow up in Christian homes and whose parents divorce—leading to inconsistent church attendance—often walk away from Christianity as adults. In addition, if the divorce takes place early in life, the parent (and the faith they profess) loses credibility in the eyes of the child. To counter this trend, Greg Popcak tells Christians, "We're going to need to get serious about promoting healthy marriages, ministering more effectively to divorced families and children-of-divorce in particular, and finding ways for our churches to be places that provide a sense of family life for members."[3] We'd like to add one more aspect to this list: As Christians, we must create more intentional relationships between parents and children in the home. The children we're raising deserve to have gospel-saturated parents/guardians who demonstrate their love by discipling them.

Disciples, not Dependents

Elicia

If we are Christ followers, we're not raising mere dependents—we're raising up disciples! Our children will do what we say for only a little while; soon they will begin doing what we do. Their eyes are watching what we do, their ears are listening to the tone we use in our conversations, and their mouths repeat what we say. Watch what you say, because if you don't, you'll watch your children say it for you!

Since we have such a great impact on our children, it's safe to say we're already discipling them indirectly with our actions. The statement "The apple doesn't fall far from the tree" is often used to describe how kids act, look, and talk like their parents. Much of this shaping doesn't happen intentionally, yet look how much they resemble us!

For example, it's eerie for me to hear our kids talk about having the same fears we had at their age—information we've never shared with them. So imagine how much we could influence our children if we intentionally instruct them according to God's Word! What we're calling for is more gospel-saturated discipleship between us as parents and the children we're raising. After all, if it's in God's will, our children will grow up and get married as well. If we set their life's rhythm to the pace of God's Word, we're creating a higher probability that they'll be more emotionally, physically, mentally, and spiritually prepared for their marriages than we were. That's a goal to work toward—reorienting our perspectives to view our children as disciples and not just dependents!

The same ingredients for discipleship that we've discussed for Christian spouses—Scripture reading and memorization, prayer, and fellowship with other saints—should be present in our relationships with our children. When we include our children in our study of God's Word, we're proactively shaping their worldview and theological understanding. This means we're beating the world to the punch!

In our family, D. A. and I chose to make the necessary sacrifices to homeschool our children. But we know that not every family is called to homeschool! Neither one of us was homeschooled growing up, but as parents we tried public and private schools in addition to homeschooling and found that the latter works best for the Horton family.

I will be honest and say that 30 to 40 percent of our instruction time is spent delivering the coursework and material. The remaining 70 to 60 percent involves dealing with each child's heart issue. D. A. and I both take Deuteronomy 6:4-9 seriously, communicating God's Word to our children throughout the day. We share a conviction to see our children not only leave the nest but also launch into the world as missionaries with a passion to reduce the hopelessness around them and help create disciples. We want them to view each gift God gives them as a tool for the mission. We tell them to consider their education advancement, future career, marriage, and family expansion through the lens of their calling to share the gospel and make disciples.

Our children need the gospel daily just as much as we do. If our children are not believers in Christ, they should be our top evangelistic prospects. If they are believers, they need the gospel to remind them of God's love for them when they sin, disappoint us, and receive our discipline.

We will be less likely to drive our children into the false idea of performing for God's love, and our love, if we practice Ephesians 6:4, which says, "Fathers, do not provoke your children to anger, but bring them up in the discipline and instruction of the Lord" (Ephesians 6:4). We can provoke our children to anger in many ways: when we withhold clear communication, when we say they're just like the spouse we bad-mouth regularly, when we demand perfection from them at all times, when we pit siblings against one another (meaning we praise one or two regularly while degrading another), and when we consistently break promises.

But we're human! We must learn to walk in humility before our children by admitting our mistakes; asking them to forgive us when we've hurt, offended, or sinned against them; and modeling for them what it looks like to walk in repentance.

Discipline

Living in a gospel-centered way as we parent our kids paves a path for us when discipline is needed. When such times arrive, we must not fall into the extremes of either being too hands-off and allowing our children to do as they please or too hands-on by physically abusing them. Neither of these extremes are acceptable nor in step with the gospel. It's always best to seek the biblical counsel of your local church leadership and holistic-discipleship team to help you make the healthiest and safest decisions regarding the loving discipline of your children.

This will provide a framework of accountability as you strive to live out the balance the apostle Paul puts forth. We see this balance in Paul's command to bring children up "in the discipline and instruction of the Lord" (Ephesians 6:4). This is a call to lovingly provide correction for erring behavior through weaving God's Word into face-to-face conversations with our children. When we discipline our children with love and concern for their souls, we're reflecting the heart of God (Hebrews 12:7-11).

In our home, D. A. and I view discipline as a tool for correction and instruction with the hope that it will lead to more consistent godly living. It's *a* tool, but not our only tool. We use discipline when our children break the rules we've set for our household. We also agreed that we will never spank our children when we're mad, and we hold each other accountable to this. This way they learn the difference between abuse and discipline. We view abuse as punishment that is unwarranted or has been given without instruction and space created for confession and repentance.

When one of our children has done something really

foolish, we tell him or her to go to a room with no electronics and wait until we say it's time to come out. The two of us will talk through the frustration we have, pray, and then decide on a form of discipline that's appropriate. Sometimes when we've been really upset, this process has taken up to an hour, and when we've gone to search out our child, he or she is fast asleep!

Our overall goal in disciplining our children is not behavior modification but heart transformation. Anyone can muster the willpower to stop a bad habit; however, only those indwelled by God the Holy Spirit can walk in a manner worthy of the gospel. There have been times we've had to call our children out for being filled with remorse (because they were caught) rather than being repentant. We've walked our older two through 2 Corinthians 7:9-11 to help them understand the difference between remorse and repentance.

We're currently walking with our oldest daughter through an ongoing issue related to technology. When we discovered a sinful behavior, she at first tried to lie and then eventually confessed. We wept together, discussed the natural consequences of her actions, and prayed together. In God's grace, she's been walking in repentance. She's told us that our time together with her in God's Word, and the way we model confessing sins before our children, spurs her to continue to confess sin rather than conceal it. This is discipleship at work. It's messy, it takes patience, and it glorifies God.

We also model this for our children by confessing our sins against them, seeking their forgiveness, and showing them our repentance by asking if they've noticed a heart change during times of frustration. Most of the time we've hurt our children's feelings by speaking harshly during times of discipline, throwing Proverbs 15:1 out the window. When we've given our children space to speak, they've told us how we confronted them using an overly harsh tone or that they were hurt when we told others what bad things they'd done. And you know what? They were right and we were wrong—and we hated when our parents did the same thing!

These types of situations stir compassion in us for our children because we can sympathize with their pain. We lead them by humbling ourselves, confessing our wrongdoing, asking them for their forgiveness, and telling them we will ask God to provide us with strength to not repeat such practices when we're disciplining them. This builds rapport and reinforces the open-door policy we've set for them to come to us anytime with anything that's on their hearts.

Making the Most of Every Opportunity

D. A.

We must always provide space for instructing our children in the ways of the Lord—we don't want them to connect godly instruction with discipline alone. Such opportunities often present themselves when our children randomly ask us loaded questions, usually during the most inconvenient times. One morning, just as I was dropping off our oldest daughter, Bella, at school, she asked, "Dad, were you a virgin when you married Mom?" Oh snap! Did my ten-year-old really just ask me that? She was looking intently at me, waiting for me to respond.

With only fifteen seconds left in our journey, I confessed to her that sadly I was not a virgin when I married Elicia—I gave my virginity away when I was an unsaved fifteen-year-old. I told her I confessed this to her mom, who forgave me for not saving myself for her. I then closed the conversation by telling Bella that when I was fifteen years old, I never imagined I'd have a ten-year-old daughter I would have to give an account to regarding my virginity. I then challenged her to learn from my sinful mistake and dedicate her body and heart to God, so that when her children ask her, she can say she remained pure before and after marriage. Bella appreciated my honesty, but I could see her disappointment over my lack of purity.

This was a teachable moment for both of us. I realized that although the gospel tells me Jesus' blood washed away my sins, I may still have to face the consequences for my sinful decisions. The gospel allows the ugliness of sinful decisions to become redeemable moments after we repent and turn our eyes toward Christ and away from our mistakes.

Elicia and I make it a habit to share honest but wise responses to our kids' questions about alcohol, drugs, pornography, and all other issues they want clarity on. We tell them that our open-door policy is in place to help us disciple them in righteousness, so they in turn will do the same.

Boxing Out Busyness

Perhaps the greatest struggle in our discipleship relationship with our children is creating space in our busy schedules to read Scripture, pray, and engage in meaningful conversations. Many Christian teens and young adults drift from their commitment to the Christian faith because the busyness of their lives ends up controlling them. And often, the home environment they were raised in cultivated this habit.

Growing up, both Elicia and I were athletes, so the competitive drive we had was channeled through sports first, and afterward we had to find space for the things of God. We've had discussions regarding how we can find balance—encouraging our children to develop passions and craft their gifts while not allowing those things to become idols. We want our children to enjoy the arts, dance, drama, and sports, but we don't want them to worship or root their identity in activities.

Fifty-seven percent of children between six and seventeen participate in at least one extracurricular activity (e.g., sports or lessons in music, language, or dance).[4] All three of our kids are in that group. We've sought to find balance by stressing the importance of honoring God by making sure we make use of our spiritual gifts while also maturing the talents He's blessed us with. The former requires a strong commitment to the local church and the latter a dedication to the activities the child is passionate about.

Often parents use the private aspect of faith as a reason not to have a strong commitment to the local church. In addition, parents worry that if their kid misses a Sunday game because of church, he or she will let teammates down or miss being seen by a scout or lose an opportunity to become a starter or participate in championship games.

Ben Zobrist, 2016 World Series MVP, would disagree with all these concerns. We engage with Ben's dad, Pastor Tom Zobrist, through gatherings at our alma mater, Calvary Bible College. Pastor Zobrist and his wife, Cindi, refused to let Ben play on teams that played on Sundays because they wanted him to "understand the importance of the local church . . . [and know] nothing is more important than the Lord." Tom also doesn't "think children make that connection if the parents don't have that commitment."[5] The Zobrists found the balance Christian parents must strive for: to remain committed to the body of Christ, all the while encouraging passion for excellence in the areas where our children are gifted.

Discipling Digital Natives

To be effective disciple-makers of our children, we must engage the technology conversation. Children today have grown up surrounded by the reality of technology. Marc Prensky calls them digital natives: those born in a digital world, speaking the "language of computers, video games and the Internet." Those not raised as digital natives, still needing to adapt to technology's advances, are digital immigrants.[6]

While many of us who are young parents are very nearly or truly digital natives ourselves, our children are engaging with technology that is different even from what we grew up with.

We need to consider ourselves as digital immigrants so we can better disciple our children in the context of a technological world. One way to do this is to find digital ways in which to communicate and connect with our children. It takes research, intentionality, and humility. But there are many resources that can help us disciple our children in the digital age.

Understanding the connection between technology and discipleship prompted me to team up with a great ministry to develop, write, and film discipleship videos contextualized in the language of urban digital natives. It was a joy to humbly partner with UYWI (Urban Youth Workers Institute) and release the *Discipleship Toolkit*.[7] This toolkit is a catalog of dozens of videos with PDF discussion questions that youth workers and even parents of teenagers can use as conversation starters. This resource has helped me even in my discipleship relationships with my own daughters.

We must pay attention to the technology our kids use and what they're engaging with so that we can maximize our opportunities for teachable moments. Elicia and I strive to do this as often as we can, whether through a pop-up advertisement on the computer, a dance craze on YouTube, or another viral video on the news. We field our kids' questions and answer them with honesty, all while directing their attention to what God's Word says about the issue.

One glaring example of this is the videos of unarmed African American men being shot by police officers and the resulting ethnic turbulence. Our kids have watched the media coverage, showing both the peaceful protests and the uproars in cities like Baltimore, Dallas, Ferguson, and Charlotte. They've asked us if the African American men in our own family could face such a fate. We're honest when we tell them that it's a possibility but that death is a guaranteed reality of sin (Romans 5:12; Hebrews 9:27) and we should pray for the salvation of those who don't know Christ. When they ask if we can trust police officers, we talk them through the fact that God ordains leaders for society and that they are held accountable to Him and we should pray for them (Romans 13:1-7; 1 Timothy 2:1-4; 1 Peter 2:13-17). We've then taken time to speak to our children about showing compassion for all families involved, encouraging them to pray for God to direct justice in each case. From here, we take it from the national to the personal level by addressing not only concerns they have but also their behavior in both public and private. These conversations then allow us to circle back to the topic of discipline and right behavior (Ephesians 6:4).

It is possible for digital immigrants to effectively disciple their digitally native children. It just takes time to identify the ways our children learn best. Sometimes a break from technology works well, while other times, using certain mediums of technology may be helpful. Either way, we must always remember not to forsake the content of Scripture, regardless of the medium. We want to explain God and His ways to our children in ways they can understand, and we must challenge them to give out what we've given them. Discipling our children provides them with ownership of their faith in Christ and leads them to a long-lasting committed relationship to their Lord and Savior.

Nonbelieving Spouses

One last pressing issue we want to address is the reality of marriages that include a spouse who has not yet accepted Jesus Christ as Savior. For the believing spouse in this situation, we pray that the gospel compels you to keep loving your spouse well. To the nonbelieving spouse, we pray that the glory of God and His goodness displayed through your spouse will point you toward embracing Christ.

This topic brings with it complex issues and questions like *How do I live with an unbelieving spouse? Can or should I divorce my unbelieving spouse? Would it be better for me to marry again, this time to a believer?* There are, of course, many nuances and unique contexts in these marriages, but Scripture provides a few principles that can encourage all who find themselves in this place.

In 1 Corinthians 7:12-16, Paul addresses the issue of Christians being married to nonbelievers. In the first verse of this passage, Paul says that if a Christian man is married to a non-Christian woman who desires to remain married, he should not divorce her. In verse 13, he provides the same counsel to a Christian woman married to an unbelieving husband. Then, in verses 14 and 16, Paul begins to lay out his reasoning: God has set apart (sanctified) the household with the believing spouse. This does not mean the unbelieving spouse is saved because he or she is married to a believer—that would be antigospel. Rather, it seems that God views the unsaved spouse and children as recipients of His ongoing grace, which is tangible through the believing spouse/parent in the home.

The believing spouse is, in effect, the living billboard of the gospel for his or her unsaved family to see day in and day out. Paul encourages each Christian to remain faithful to his or her unsaved spouse and children so that the grace of God and His goodness will draw them to repentance (Romans 2:4). Living with and loving an unbelieving spouse is a work of evangelism. None of us are omniscient; we're unaware if and when our spiritual deposits take root. But we serve a God who grants repentance to those who are currently not saved, and when they come to a "knowledge of the truth" (2 Timothy 2:25), the Holy Spirit regenerates them (John 3:3-8) so they are alive in Christ (2 Corinthians 5:17; Ephesians 2:4-10).

However, in verse 15 Paul provides clarity regarding a situation in which the unbelieving spouse abandons the believing spouse. If this is the case, Paul tells the believer to let him or her go. The heart behind this is to live out Romans 12:18, which says, "If possible, so far as it depends on you, live peaceably with all." Paul says that when the unbelieving spouse abandons the marriage (files for divorce), the Christian is no longer under the vows of the marriage because the unbeliever has legally broken them. Some say the Christian is not free to remarry; others say he or she is free to remarry another believer. We agree with the latter, especially if the believer is struggling sexually by burning with lust (1 Corinthians 7:9). However, for specific situations,

IT STARTS AT HOME

it's always best to seek the biblical counsel of your local church leadership and holistic-discipleship team before making decisions regarding divorce and remarriage.

The Gospel-Saturated Home

The Christian home is an embassy of heaven on earth. It should be a safe place for correction, fun, healing, instruction, sanctuary, and training. At the same time, the Christian home is a bunker—a place of refuge when we're under attack from all sides. Knowing this, we should be driven to see the gospel saturate every interpersonal relationship in the Christian home. There should be a discipleship rhythm between spouses and children. Our goal should be to see each of our family members love God, carry the light of the gospel into our world, and pursue a life of holiness. Second Timothy 3:16 tells us Scripture is here "for training in righteousness." There's no better place than the Christian home to work out our faith with our spouses and children.

CHAPTER 6

CAN WE STAY PURE?

Let marriage be held in honor among all, and let the marriage bed be
undefiled, for God will judge the sexually immoral and adulterous.

HEBREWS 13:4

D. A.

As Christians, we're told that sexual purity is something we strive for prior to marriage. "Save yourself for your spouse," people say. The implication, therefore, is that the need for purity ends at marriage. After all, it's what we've remained pure for, right? But here's a profound truth: Marriage is not the cure for fornication, lust, or pornography. The gospel is. And the need for purity doesn't end once we're married, because although sex is indeed a beautiful part of marriage, the heart issues that inform purity (or the lack thereof) remain the same.

Not many who enter into the covenant of marriage

understand the reality of gospel purity before taking their vows. Elicia and I were one such couple. We thought we had accomplished the goal of sexual purity once we said "I do." But we didn't consider the sexual baggage we brought into our marriage and the obstacles that baggage would place in our path as we traveled down the road of intimacy together. For us, the battle to remain sexually pure in marriage became just as important as our pursuit of purity prior to marriage.

We're more convinced now than we've ever been that remaining pure in marriage is vital. God created boundaries for His children even within the framework of sexuality because He knows the severity of the consequences of sin.

Consensual premarital sex brings momentary pleasure— we rarely hear anyone say otherwise. Sex is enjoyable; it's supposed to be. God created it for us to enjoy! However, we frequently hear from people who are struggling with the spiritual, physical, mental, and emotional consequences of seeking sexual pleasure outside the boundaries of marriage. What often results is sexual brokenness and separation between spouses, preventing couples from being on the same page in the areas of sexual experience, expectations, and enjoyment.

A gospel-saturated marriage possesses a holistic ethic of sexual purity during marriage, regardless of whether it was present before marriage vows were exchanged. A holistic ethic infuses each spouse with a desire to build guardrails around their marriage to protect them from wandering into the attractive world of sexual immorality. Christians can pursue and find sexual purity within a gospel-saturated marriage. As with so much of following God's way in marriage, it takes hard work, sacrifice, and commitment to God and to each other, but the blessings of a sexually pure marriage are worth it.

Boundaries and Freedom

Elicia

Our family loves sports. We favor basketball and baseball and try to take our kids to professional games when we can. And when we visit Dodger Stadium, we know the baseball game is not taking place in the parking lot or in the stands but rather on the baseball field. If a ball goes outside the set boundaries, it's considered a foul ball. The boundaries in baseball allow the game to be played fairly and freely enjoyed.

In a similar way, sexual intimacy inside the God-given boundaries is freeing and enjoyable. Genesis 2:24-25 lays the theological groundwork for God's design for sexual intimacy: Sexual intercourse is to be between one man and one woman inside the covenant of marriage. This sexual encounter, when not forced or defiled by sinful practices, is beautiful. The sexual relationship should include only a husband and wife who have committed themselves to each other (Proverbs 5:15-19; Song of Songs 7:6-12; Matthew 5:28; Mark 10:6-9; 1 Thessalonians 4:3-5). As an added blessing, God designed sexual intimacy as the potential means for couples to procreate (Genesis 4:1).

Practically speaking, D. A. and I see sexual boundaries

in marriage intersecting with two passages of Scripture: 1 Corinthians 7:2-5 and Hebrews 13:4. In 1 Corinthians 7:2-5 Paul says,

> Because of the temptation to sexual immorality, each man should have his own wife and each woman her own husband. The husband should give to his wife her conjugal rights, and likewise the wife to her husband. For the wife does not have authority over her own body, but the husband does. Likewise the husband does not have authority over his own body, but the wife does. Do not deprive one another, except perhaps by agreement for a limited time, that you may devote yourselves to prayer; but then come together again, so that Satan may not tempt you because of your lack of self-control.

In this passage Paul advocates for monogamy in the marriage relationship between one husband and one wife.[1] In verses 2-4 Paul speaks about the freedom in sexual intimacy between husbands and wives. The driving reason for this freedom is to avoid sexual immorality. Paul's language becomes challenging when he speaks of the sexual rights of each spouse. Paul is actually calling for equal rights in sexual intimacy: One spouse does not have all rights while the other is subservient. Each spouse should willingly give themselves in mutual submission as a gift to each other every time they are sexually intimate.

Hebrews 13:4 also informs our framework of holistic purity: "Let marriage be held in honor among all, and let the marriage bed be undefiled, for God will judge the sexually immoral and adulterous." The word *undefiled* means to be "pure in a . . . moral sense."[2] It is the same word used in Hebrews 7:26 to describe the sinless and perfect life of Jesus Christ during His incarnation.[3] Paul Ellingworth says keeping the marriage bed pure means for the married couple to "keep themselves exclusively for one another, or incur God's judgment."[4] Each married couple should work together to keep their sexual relationship pure by not emotionally or sexually opening up their marriage to anyone else. Conversations about struggles and temptations should take place between spouses before either shares with someone else, particularly someone of the opposite gender. Healthy communication is key to keeping the marriage bed undefiled.

Communicate, Communicate, Communicate

D. A.

What does communication that keeps the marriage bed undefiled look like? We've already talked about how communication is key in a gospel-saturated marriage. And this communication should extend to talking about sexual intimacy. In our marriage, Elicia and I have an understanding that sex is not something either of us should demand but rather something we should both mutually pursue and enjoy. This sounds great; however, men and women are often not on the same page in this pursuit. This reality has caused times of frustration in our marriage. Sometimes I wanted sexual intimacy when Elicia was tired and ready to go to sleep—and sex was the furthest thought from her mind. Or because we didn't communicate much or connect emotionally during the day, she wasn't ready to connect physically. She desired holistic intimacy, and I wanted physical intimacy.

Sometimes Elicia would stay awake so we could be intimate, and I would tell her to just go to sleep because I thought she was staying up only to allow me to fulfill my sexual desires. She would get frustrated, but I felt it was selfish for me alone to receive pleasure while she "took one for the team." Communication has been vital in our relationship because we're tempted to protect ourselves from being hurt, prioritizing our insecurities over intimacy with each other.

Spouses need to be honest in their communication as they work toward mutual submission; only then will sexual intimacy be a beautiful and enjoyable experience and not an exasperating burden. Being open in our communication helps protect our hearts, minds, and bodies from the ways the world might tempt us to meet our sexual needs.

For Elicia and me, developing a level of comfort with talking through our sexual needs took time. At first, we felt awkward in speaking transparently about our sex life and embarrassed as we asked each other questions. However, we just took our time and laughed our way through most of the initial conversations. It wasn't until our fifth year of marriage that our communication about sexuality went to conversation level one. Reaching this level of openness with your spouse, sharing and addressing the most difficult aspects of your sexuality, is vital to reaching true intimacy.

Acknowledge the Broken Places

Elicia

None of us comes to marriage without some level of sexual brokenness, whether because of choices we have made or because of things that were done against us. These things are barriers to intimacy, and the only way to break down those barriers is to be vulnerable with our pain and broken places. Healing can only happen through intentional pursuit, both through openness with our spouses and humility about places of sin.

Both D. A. and I have dealt with discomfort in our sexual intimacy because of traumatic sexual experiences as well as periodic ongoing struggles in our marriage. When I was in second grade, I was cornered and assaulted by two of my classmates. I was too young and too terrified to even speak up about what happened. They threatened to harm me if I ever told a soul. As we shared in chapter 3, the very first person I ever told was D. A., in our fifth year of marriage. We were working through an awkward conversation about sexual difficulties we were having, and he just didn't understand why I was so uncomfortable with him even touching me. I really didn't understand either—until we started going deeper in our conversation. It was then I realized that my sexual assault had everything to do with why I never enjoyed being embraced by my husband. I never enjoyed his touch. I never welcomed it. I always felt violated. I was a twenty-six-year-old married woman who could not enjoy the freedom of sexual intimacy with my husband. Because of a violation I'd experienced when I was young and innocent, I was living in bondage.

This traumatic childhood experience eventually plunged me into a secret world of being addicted to pornography, masturbating, and seeking attention from boys. I didn't realize how emotionally unstable the assault had made me until I was in seminary taking counseling courses. I praise God that through my pursuit of education, He was priming my heart to find healing. I had forgiven my attackers, but because I had lived in fear and mental torment for so many years, I hadn't realized that I'd never asked God to heal me. As D. A. and I both opened our hearts that day, we were able to make ourselves vulnerable to each other and enjoy a new level of sexual intimacy because of how deep we went in our conversation.

D. A.

Elicia's transparency helped bring to light issues in my own heart. A neighbor had exposed me to pornography when I was six years old, and the images of that video are still burned in my memory—I can never unsee them. Because I grew up in an environment where masculinity was measured by one's sexual prowess, pornography and older teens became my tutors. By the time I lost my virginity at fifteen, my entire life was driven by a single goal: to get constant attention from as many girls as possible.

During our growing-up years, Elicia always rejected my attempts to get her attention. Because of this, I viewed her with a measure of respect that I sadly didn't have for other girls. She possessed an innocence that I held in high regard. Since the age of ten I'd tried to win her affections, but my immature ways always proved to be counterproductive. I would regularly ask her if she wanted to go out with friends of mine from my neighborhood, trying to get her to confess that she liked me, not them. She always declined and never indicated she had feelings for me.

During our vulnerable conversation about sexuality, Elicia told me she grew frustrated with my methods because I made her feel promiscuous. My heart sank as I heard this. I shared with Elicia that I longed for her to pursue me and tell me she wanted me, and that this desire had never left. Having Elicia pursue me physically and verbally would be a win-win because she would be expressing both of my love languages. But my struggle with pornography distorted my view of sex.

Today it's easier to access porn on a cell phone than it is to get milk from your own fridge. Because of this accessibility, many marriages are suffering. Porn addiction is a painful form of sexual impurity that undermines the good sexual ethic God created for marriage. However, Christian marriages face an uphill battle when it comes to pornography. The pendulum of American culture has shifted, and porn is now viewed as acceptable and normative. In fact, some couples have invited pornography into their bedroom to "spice things up"—but are now facing the consequences of a developed addiction.

Because both Elicia and I, even as believers in Christ, have struggled with pornography, its consequences have tainted the way we viewed sexuality. We're finding healing only by God's grace and through the accountability structures of a small circle of brothers and sisters in the Lord. Grace and accountability are not automatically guaranteed to prevent someone from falling into the trap of pornography; rather, they provide strength during times of temptation and the freedom to confess when lapses into sin take place.

I'm going to be completely vulnerable and share how grace and accountability have informed my own struggles with this. One night in 2010, around eleven, Elicia was in the bathroom getting ready for bed, and the door between us was closed. As I was flipping through channels, I stopped and watched a pornographic scene on Showtime for a minute. I grew convicted and changed the channel right as Elicia opened the door. Immediately the embarrassment crushed me, and all the blood in my body rushed to my face. Elicia asked what was wrong, and I lied and said, "Nothing."

The next morning I woke up early to pray and confess my sin. For a few months prior to this, a group of men in our church would text each other every morning to report our victory, or failure, regarding pornography (and other sexual sin) from the day before. This was the first time I was going to confess a sin to our group, and I knew I also had to confess to Elicia when she woke up. I sent a lengthy text message to the group and then went to record a podcast. During the podcast I opened up about my recent fall into looking at porn and then saved the file to my computer. When I logged off, I noticed that my phone had dozens of notifications. Something wasn't right. It was only six thirty in the morning! No one ever contacted me so early unless it was a pastoral emergency. As I scrolled through my phone, I saw they were notifications from Facebook regarding responses to a status I'd apparently posted more than an hour before. I was puzzled. I hadn't posted anything to Facebook—had I?

I quickly logged on to Facebook, and I couldn't believe what I saw. My text message to my accountability group had somehow been posted to my Facebook page instead! Thousands of people had viewed what I thought I had sent to my small inner circle of accountability partners. People were leaving mixed reviews about my confession—some were very supportive and thanked me for being a pastor who is honest about his struggle; others shamed me for openly confessing; and others told me I needed to put accountability structures in place.

I removed the Facebook post, went upstairs, and confessed to Elicia all that had happened the night before and that morning. She forgave me, telling me she knew I had been lying but trusted the Lord to bring me to a place of confession and repentance. I felt as though I were disqualified for the pastorate, but both my wife and elders (who were in my circle of accountability) said that my confession and desire to remain accountable were a sign of victory in this area and would serve as adequate fruit of repentance.

One redemptive and unforeseen outcome from my fall into sin was the number of single and married men who approached me after the fact, confessing their deep addictions to porn. I had heard of men struggling with this addiction, but I had never known how deep of an impact it was having on men in the body of Christ. Over the course of time, Elicia and I were both asked to counsel married men and women who struggled not only with an addiction to porn but also with the defilement and damage to their marriage bed.

Many men who struggle with pornography are unable to physically engage in sexual activity because of a medical condition known as PIED (Porn-Induced Erectile Dysfunction). The women in these marriages struggle with feelings of inadequacy. Over time, due to a lack of communication, confession, and repentance, the married couple begins to drift away from each other in every other area of life, and sadly they transition into roommates on the verge of divorce. It's important to note that porn addiction is a struggle not just for men but also for women. In recent years, the number of married women who are addicted to porn is rising and must be considered as well.[5]

Again, married couples can keep the destruction of pornography at bay if they openly communicate their struggles with it and seek victory over it. Identifying the root causes for this addiction is crucial, and spouses must confess, extend forgiveness, and put an accountability structure in place. Married couples must cling to the cross of Christ and love each other through times of confession and forgiveness as well as through times of victory.

Applying the Gospel to Sexual Purity

Elicia

Being vulnerable about sexual brokenness and seeking healing together allows married couples to move forward in greater intimacy. For D. A. and me, understanding our areas of brokenness helped each of us reconsider our individual approaches to sexual intimacy. We gained a better grasp of what we each carried into our marriage. This perspective and healing meant we better understood the sexual rights we each possessed and also gave us direction on how we could steward each other's bodies in a way that glorified God and honored each other. We now work on communicating with clarity about sexual intimacy while also leaving room for spontaneity.

As you and your spouse seek to cultivate healthy sexual intimacy in your marriage, communicate your desire for holistic intimacy, beyond just physical pleasure. D. A. and I have learned to connect relationally and emotionally so that I can enjoy our time. As he is intentional to not rush the process, I'm able to mentally fight through the scars from my childhood and freely give myself without feeling guilty. This helps me communicate to D. A. that I find him attractive and desire him, affirming that he is meeting my needs.

Fighting for purity in marriage means committing to asking the tough questions and being willing to answer honestly. D. A. and I have developed a rhythm of conversation when it comes to our purity in marriage. We first tell each other that we have remained pure by not allowing our bodies, hearts, and minds to entertain or pursue a person of the same or opposite gender. We then ask each other directly if we have remained faithful to our vows. This is an uncomfortable, vulnerable question because there's always the potential for one of us (or both) to say that we have defiled the marriage bed.

But these conversations are incredibly valuable. First, if one or both of us is struggling with sin, we can confess and seek spiritual restoration through the leadership in our local church (1 John 1:8-10; Galatians 6:1-2). Second, if we have no sin to confess, we're reassured of our love and dedication to each other. And third, the conversation helps us assess our commitment to the gospel and how we apply it in the most intimate area of our marriage: our sexuality. A gospel-saturated marriage calls both spouses to submit their past, present, and future concerns to the Lord while walking together in sexual freedom within God's boundaries.

If you seek healing and want sexual purity in your marriage, there are many gospel-saturated resources out there to equip husbands and wives. Of course, the greatest resource any of us has is Scripture. Matthew 5:29-30 says, "If your right eye causes you to sin, tear it out and throw it away.

For it is better that you lose one of your members than that your whole body be thrown into hell. And if your right hand causes you to sin, cut it off and throw it away. For it is better that you lose one of your members than that your whole body go into hell." This passage shows Jesus' radical approach to sin. Now, this passage is not saying we should literally maim ourselves to fight the sin of lust. After all, gouging out an eye or cutting off a hand does not remove lust from the human heart. What Jesus is calling His followers to do is to deal with sin quickly by attacking its root. Dr. Thomas Constable points us to the counsel of D. A. Carson, who reminds believers that sin begins in the imagination, and believers who desire to pursue Kingdom righteousness must dwell on what is found in Philippians 4:8 instead of unholy thoughts.[6]

As married couples, we must discern what feeds our imaginations and tempts our hearts to stray from sexual purity. This includes the movies and TV shows we watch, the music we listen to, the text messages we exchange, and the pictures we look at on Instagram. It could also be regular private conversations in which we make deep emotional investments in people other than our spouses. If we're going to take Jesus' radical approach, we must work to purify our thought life by cutting out everything that's tempting our hearts to drift away from the counsel of Philippians 4:8.

The gospel reminds us "that Christ died for our sins in accordance with the Scriptures" (1 Corinthians 15:3). Therefore, the sin of lust and all the sinful practices we use to feed it have been dealt with by our Savior, who rose from the grave in victory over them (verse 4). Ephesians 1:7 says, "In him we have redemption through his blood, the forgiveness of our trespasses, according to the riches of his grace," which means that God is not stingy with forgiveness because the shed blood of Christ has bought us out of sin's slavery and paid our debt in full! This truth should encourage couples to work together to keep any area of sexual sin from forcing them back into a place of slavery, because in Christ we're free from the bondage of sin—we are dead to it, and it is no longer our master (Romans 6:1-14).

Romans 12:1-2 calls each of us to seek the Holy Spirit's work in transforming us after we've surrendered our whole being to God as a living sacrifice. There's power when a married couple comes together in prayer to surrender themselves holistically to God for His glory. This practice results in their good (Romans 8:28).

Couples should also work together to memorize Scripture since, as we've talked about before, quoting God's Word is how we use the offensive weapon of the armor He's given us (Ephesians 6:17). Psalm 119:11 says, "I have stored up your word in my heart, that I might not sin against you." We must not only memorize the Word of God but also quote it when we're tempted and then live out the application daily (James 1:22-25). Scripture is a tool of sanctification from God to us (John 17:16-19).

In addition to leaning on Scripture, each married couple who struggles to keep their marriage bed pure should seek counseling from their local pastor or a counselor. This person can help them employ healthy practices that ensure accountability, authentic communication, and sexual faithfulness. Couples struggling with pornography can also install accountability software such as Covenant Eyes. This service also offers rich resources to help believers walk in victory over porn.[7] Another resource, Paul Maxwell's article "Seven Things to Do After You Look at Pornography,"[8] can help with returning to a biblical view of God and also lays out a plan for confession, repentance, and restoration.

No matter the damage our past sexual experiences or sins have caused, the gospel's implications comfort us. Borrowing from the title of an Andraé Crouch song, "The blood [of Jesus] will never lose its power"![9] Second Corinthians 1:3-7 commissions us to comfort those who are afflicted. So when you begin to vulnerably share your sexual experiences, your victimization, or your participation in sinfulness, may you be led by the Holy Spirit to love and embrace your spouse as Christ has embraced you. When you said "I do," you said "I do" to the whole person you committed your life to—and he or she agreed to accept you with all your baggage as well.

When sin is exposed in a gospel-saturated marriage, each spouse is reassured of the forgiveness, grace, and peace that accompany our fruits of repentance (2 Corinthians 7:9-11), continued growth in Christ (2 Corinthians 3:18), and the promise of glorification (Romans 8:29-30). It is possible to fight for sexual purity in marriage and be victorious when Christ dwells in the hearts of both spouses and each submits his or her whole life to Him. Being in gospel-saturated marriages equips us to win battles against lust, to set up a rhythm of healthy communication, and to create a system of accountability. All of this allows us to live out a oneness that reflects the very nature of the God we serve! Imagine the witness we could have before our world if we as believers kept our marriage beds undefiled while enjoying the freedom we have for sexual intimacy within the boundaries God has set.

CHAPTER 7

ON THE ROPES

Remove far from me falsehood and lying; give me neither poverty nor riches; feed me with the food that is needful for me, lest I be full and deny you and say, "Who is the LORD?" or lest I be poor and steal and profane the name of my God.

PROVERBS 30:8-9

D. A.

Finances put a strain on marriages. It's the leading cause of stress in marriage,[1] and one researcher says that arguing about money is a top predictor of divorce.[2] We're stressed because we typically come to marriage with different ideas about how to handle finances! In a survey by SunTrust, 47 percent of those polled said they have different spending patterns than their partner, and 35 percent admitted the top reason for their relational stress was caused by finances.[3]

Elicia and I have already admitted that we have different philosophies when it comes to spending or saving money, but we've realized it's foolish not to talk about money simply because it leads to arguments. The tension that comes with discussing money is an opportunity for togetherness that cultivates a culture of generosity inside our home. When we establish a culture of generosity, money is no longer an idol or a wedge of division but instead a tool that can be used for God's glory.

We are by no means perfect when it comes to finances, and we're still learning. We had major financial struggles early in our marriage, and while we had a great rhythm from 2008 through 2015, our entire philosophy of generosity was completely restructured and rebuilt on Scripture after our church-planting residency in 2015.

In this chapter we will unveil what is, perhaps outside of sexuality, the most guarded and intimate insight to a household: the financial picture. We will walk through mistakes we've endured and victories we've shared over almost fifteen years of marriage. We will unpack Scriptures that support a biblical philosophy of money. And we will examine dos and don'ts for a family budget as well as provide a mock budget sheet and shopping list for you and your spouse to work through. Healthy finances are meant to be practical and achievable, and a gospel-saturated marriage puts finances in their proper place.

Filing for Chapter 7

A few days before our first daughter, Izabelle, was born, we moved out of our first apartment and into Elicia's parents' house. We were trying to save for a down payment on a house of our own, and within six months we had enough. We consulted a lender, received our credit background checks, and were told we had $189,000 to spend. We were floored! Never in our wildest dreams had we thought we would be preapproved for such a high figure. We were both filled with an overwhelming sense of pride. Our combined annual salaries totaled less than $50,000, neither of us had a college degree, and the house I grew up in was valued at only $18,000! We felt as though we'd hit the jackpot and immediately began shopping.

We found a three-bedroom, two-bathroom condo we liked that was not too far from our immediate families. But the day before we were going to sign the contract, my mother-in-law told us that her next-door neighbor's house was for sale. We did a walk-through and immediately fell in love! It had three bedrooms, two and a half bathrooms, a finished basement, a screened-in back porch, and a backyard that would be great for our kids to play in. In addition to being next door to Elicia's mom and dad, it was across the street from Elicia's brother, his wife, and their kids. It was the perfect setup for these two kids who grew up in the hood and wanted to finally have their shot at living the American dream.

The neighbor sold us the house as is without going through a Realtor—for only $119,000! It had appraised for $135,000, and we realized we would be foolish to pass this up. The very next day we contacted a family friend to draw up the paperwork, and at the ages of twenty-three and twenty-two we were homeowners.

Quickly we began to do renovation projects, and the bills

began to rack up. The first time we tried to fill the swimming pool, a pipe burst and our basement flooded. Home insurance didn't cover the cost, and we realized we needed to bite the bullet and redo the basement. We decided to exhaust the equity in our house to pay for the needed renovations. The money we received from the bank allowed us to not only redo our basement but also lay asphalt, put a basketball court in the backyard, and purchase equipment for a home recording studio. We then used the remaining money for other small projects around the house, down payments for new cars, and family vacations.

A year later, however, Elicia was laid off from her job. We had no idea that she would not be able to find work for another two years. At first we didn't fret because we still had money in our savings account. What we did not understand was this was borrowed money, not money that was ours. When our savings began to deplete, we contacted another bank about a second mortgage. They appraised our house and with all the home improvements said they would finance us for a loan of $20,000. We took the second mortgage, and this was the straw, added to the multitudes under it, that broke the camel's back.

After we received the check for the second mortgage, we told ourselves we were going to cut back on our recreational spending—only to take more family trips and put money down on a time-share in Florida. Needless to say, over the next eighteen months our savings went from $20,000 of borrowed money down to $200. We were in over our heads but were too prideful to admit it. Little did we know we weren't alone in this; all around the United States people were living beyond their means and losing their homes.

One night we talked through the possibility of filing for bankruptcy, which led to an argument that caused us to consider the condition of our marriage. We did not agree to file bankruptcy and instead decided to take matters into our own hands by having weekly garage sales, and in church on Sundays we'd ask God to get us out of our financial predicament. One time, Elicia even tried out for the TV show *Deal or No Deal* in an attempt to pay off our debt! We also dropped a hundred dollars on Powerball tickets when the jackpot was more than $200 million. We said if we didn't win, we'd never spend money on lottery tickets again. Obviously we didn't win, and to this day, we've kept our promise.

Our overall goal was to keep our house so that we could look like we were living the American dream, but in reality what we were living was a nightmare. After a few months of our prayers not being answered in the way we had hoped and not being able to sell enough stuff to pay the bills, we came to a realization: There was no possible way to pay off what we had racked up from both of our mortgages, our credit card bills, and the consequences of our frivolous spending habits. We met with a bankruptcy lawyer, giving him all the necessary documents, and a week later he counseled us to file for Chapter 7 bankruptcy.

Chapter 7 allowed us to walk away from all our debt outside of student loans. We qualified for Chapter 7 because of our low income—I was the only one working. Our income-to-debt ratio was embarrassing, and filing for bankruptcy helped us realize we'd been living in idolatry.

The next few years were humbling, to say the least. We walked away from our home and moved into an apartment that was infested with mold and cockroaches. We went from our gorgeous dream house to a thousand-square-foot apartment with two bedrooms and one bathroom. Our fifty-one-inch big-screen TV was replaced by a thirteen-inch Disney Princess–themed TV we borrowed from our daughter.

We canceled all our credit cards, paid cash for necessities, and, for the first time, began giving financially to our local church on a consistent basis. This level of humility brought us closer together, and during this necessary season we made repentance a lifestyle—not something we only practiced in the midst of crisis. We aren't embarrassed to share our story because doing so has allowed other couples to match our vulnerability and share their previous and current financial struggles. Only by owning the weight of financial struggles in marriage and being willing to talk about them can we find the togetherness to move forward.

Culture of Generosity

We could start by talking about the healthy financial practices we began to use after filing bankruptcy, but we need to first talk about what takes priority. As Christians, the way we handle our finances should emerge from our hearts—how God has called us to be. That's why we have to start with the principle that the Christian home needs to have a dominant culture of generosity. We learned about this during our season in the church-planting residency at Summit Church. During our time there, Pastor J. D. Greear and the entire team of elders and leaders launched the Multiply initiative,[4] a two-year church-wide generosity project that would seek to accomplish two tasks: (1) see 100 percent of church members encountering God in a way that redefines their view of generosity, and (2) raise more than $50 million for Summit's aggressive global church-planting strategy.

J. D. would regularly say that even if one donor would give the entire $50 million, the primary goal of the Multiply initiative would still need to be met! The heart behind this message quickly showed me that the initiative was not about the money—it was about every member of Summit Church doing what was necessary to create and foster a culture of generosity.

The culture of generosity can be framed around what J. D. called the Generosity Matrix.[5] He said there are two extremes for how Christians view their relationship with their possessions. The first is that God wants only 10 percent, and we can do what we want with the other 90 percent. The problem with this view is that it turns God into a servant we use to try to gain more wealth. (If we honor Him by giving 10 percent, He is forced to bless us with more.) The second extreme is that God's only intention for us having money is to give it all away. This position lacks balance because there's an end to how much we're supposed to give. Additionally, this position gives room for what Paul called compulsory giving, which involves a person giving because they feel forced to give rather than giving freely (2 Corinthians 8–9).

The Generosity Matrix helps us identify a middle-of-the-road approach to our financial stewardship of all that God gives us. This matrix is composed of six principles:

1. *God gives excess to some so that they may share with those who have less.*
   Second Corinthians 8:13-15 is a picture of how we should not hoard the excess we have; rather, we should share it with those we know have need. Sharing is the reason God provides us with excess.

2. *Jesus' radical generosity toward us should motivate us to be radical in our generosity toward others.*
   In 2 Corinthians 8–9, Paul uses Jesus' sacrifice as a model for how believers should give to those in need. As God provides us with more resources, we should steward the new resources to help others.

3. *The Holy Spirit is the one who should guide the sacrifices we make.*
   Romans 8:14 says that "all who are led by the Spirit of God are sons of God," and John 16:13 says that the Holy Spirit "will guide [believers] into all the truth." We must be sensitive to the leading of the Holy Spirit so we won't miss opportunities to extend generosity to others.

4. *God delights in our enjoyment of the material gifts He provides to us.*

   First Timothy 6:17-19 says that God is the one who "provides us with everything to enjoy." This principle must not be isolated from the other five; if it is, we'll be prone to pursue the pleasures of this life, including the things that are not pleasing to God. Keep this principle grouped with the other five in order to walk in balance.

5. *We should never place our trust in riches or define our lives by the things we have.*

   In Matthew 6:25-33 Jesus speaks to two groups. To the first He says that God will provide better security than money, and to the second He says that God, not money, makes their lives significant. When God is the source of our security and significance, our giving to Him will be worship, not a tip. God doesn't want to be tipped like a waiter—He wants to be worshiped!

6. *Wealth building is actually good.*

   The book of Proverbs provides plenty of examples of how wealth building is a good thing. Proverbs 13:22 says, "A good man leaves an inheritance to his children's children." Proverbs such as 3:9-10; 10:22; 14:24; and 21:5 all speak to wealth building as something positive.

All six of these principles need to be kept together. If they aren't, our approach to money will be out of balance, and we will slide to one of the two extremes mentioned earlier. After hearing this teaching, Elicia and I decided to pray and seek the Lord as a couple with God's view of generosity in mind.

To be a part of the Summit Network residency during this season, I willingly took a $20,000-a-year pay cut. Elicia and I felt it was worth it because the experiences and investments we would receive couldn't be measured by dollars and cents. I share this with you so you can see how our prayers regarding God's view of generosity were answered. Immediately the Lord began to put both of our hearts on the same page regarding the Generosity Matrix, and we began to pray through opportunities to give beyond what we were already giving regularly to our local church.

First, we felt led to support two church-planting families. Since we were about to reenter the church-planting world, where fund-raising is a must, we wanted to bless other families who were already in that tension. We knew how urban church planters struggled at a unique level, so we were mindful to select families who were running to plant in areas most people generally ran from. We contacted one family who was planting in Miami and another who was going to Houston. We told both families that we were going to support them monthly for a year. Needless to say, they were blessed to hear the news, and they knew the sacrifice we were making since we, too, were preparing to plant. We told them our hearts were leading us to support them as they planted the gospel in needy communities.

Second, we decided to anonymously bless families who were struggling to pay their bills. To a single mother who needed help paying rent and buying food and clothes for her kids, we sent a gift with a note expressing the giver as God—because He's the one who had placed her story in our pathway. We also made financial contributions to other families as well.

Last, we decided to support three children through Compassion International. Each of our children would sponsor a child, who would also become a pen pal. We wanted to put faces to the sacrificial contributions we were making so our children could better connect with these precious souls. We also challenged our kids to commit to a pattern of intercessory prayer for these children.

The Generosity Matrix wasn't just content we were introduced to; it was a life-altering framework we were challenged to put in place for our household. To God's glory, we desire to leverage the excess we have for the benefit of our marriage, our children, the body of Christ, and evangelistic efforts to reach the lost. We now share the same intentional language of Summit Church with our children, so that when we launch them into the world as missionaries, their hearts will be inclined to live out generosity in greater ways.

Gospel-saturated marriages thrive in home environments where a culture of generosity is the norm. Even after I took a substantial pay cut, we were able to serve as a blessing to those in need because God still somehow provided excess. Revealing the ways in which we were blessed to give to those in need is not so we can receive rewards or recognition; rather, it is to honor the God who provided us with the gifts that we could share with others.

The Generosity Matrix calls husbands and wives to come face-to-face with each other and the Lord regarding how they are to steward the financial resources He has provided them with. The matrix also provides a plan that helps couples figure out how they can share generously with those in need, pay bills on time, live within their means, carve out funds for recreation, and save with the intention of blessing their children. Consider working through the Generosity Matrix with your spouse, and pray together about implementing it or another strategy for financial accountability.

A Biblical Philosophy on Stewardship of Money

Now that we've laid the framework of a culture of generosity, we want to unpack a few key Scripture verses that have helped us develop a biblical philosophy concerning the stewardship of money. Stewardship is the joint organization and managing of resources—and it is something Elicia and I work on together in all areas of life. In our home, stewardship involves managing our family calendar, interpersonal relationships, home repairs, children's needs, and, of course, finances. Financial stewardship includes assessing what we have coming in, what's going out, and how we're doing with our goals (such as emergency savings and our kids' savings accounts). Scripture provides important insights about financial stewardship.

The first passage we're going to look at is Proverbs 30:8-9, which says, "Remove far from me falsehood and lying; give me neither poverty nor riches; feed me with the food that is needful for me, lest I be full and deny you and say, 'Who is the LORD?' or lest I be poor and steal and profane the name of my God." This passage identifies a necessary ingredient of a biblical philosophy of stewardship: having a heart that is content.

In this proverb we see the cry for stewardship. The author asks God to preserve a life of integrity for him that is lived out by being neither rich nor poor. During times of abundance, we assume that our wealth has been accumulated because of individual giftedness, strength, and determination. In contrast, when we lack finances, we are tempted to do anything necessary to earn money to meet our basic needs. During both extremes, the heart is tempted to forget about God and act as if He isn't relevant. A heart of contentment safeguards us from forgetting about God when we have much or when we have little. The ultimate concern of the author of this proverb was holy living before God. A heart of contentment remains grateful for all that God has provided while rejecting the temptations that result from being wealthy or poor.

During our marriage, Elicia and I have had seasons of plenty as well as seasons of, in all honesty, next to nothing. There were times when we gifted, not loaned, money to others who were in need and times when people both gifted and loaned money to us. Filing for bankruptcy before celebrating our fifth anniversary of marriage recalibrated our hearts to first ask God to make us content and second to prompt us to obey Him with our spending. This was such a turning point in our marriage that we now recognize the truth of Psalm 37:25-26, in which David expresses he has "not seen the righteous forsaken"! We used to quote this verse, but we weren't living it—we were not operating in obedience to God with our finances. We literally had to start over so we could handle our finances in a way that was honoring to God and not self-serving.

The second passage we want to unpack is Matthew 6:31-33, which says, "Do not be anxious, saying, 'What shall we eat?' or 'What shall we drink?' or 'What shall we wear?' For the Gentiles seek after all these things, and your heavenly Father knows that you need them all. But seek first the kingdom of God and his righteousness, and all these things will be added to you." This passage speaks to the way we view God as being the supplier of our needs. Dr. Thomas Constable says, "Since God provides so bountifully for His own, it is not only foolish but pagan to fret about the basic necessities of life. The fretting disciple lives as an unbeliever (Gentile) who disbelieves and disregards God. Such a person devotes too much of his or her attention to the accumulation of material goods, and disregards the more important things in life."[6]

Christians are to trust in the providing hands of God over everything else. We must live in a posture of surrender—offering all our needs to God, who has a proven track record of supplying everything we need. Jesus Himself is saying that God, who is sovereign over all things, knows what we need and will provide us with the basic necessities: food, water, and clothing.

The heart of biblical stewardship includes not only contentment but also a trust in God rather than self. The temptation we face regularly is the impulse to put our trust in things, not God—our jobs, checking and savings accounts, limits on credit cards, equity in our homes, and retirement portfolios (if we have a strategy for retirement). Sometimes we aren't aware that our trust is in these things until they are gone.

Early in our marriage, Elicia and I both had regular seasons of unemployment, and we would seek God for His intervention—but sadly, when we found employment and our savings accounts added a comma, we would lose our desire to trust in Him. We continued to fall into the trap of trusting in our own interview skills, employment opportunities, and savings account. God was not the bedrock of our trust. Consequently, our hearts never really became content with what we had. We always wanted more.

In hindsight, we praise God for the crash of our finances because it took something that drastic to stop trusting in ourselves and to start trusting God—in good financial times and bad. Each employment opportunity we receive, each financial crisis we emerge from, and every move we make is with an attitude of gratefulness to God as our provider. Now, we place Kingdom principles in the forefront of our decision-making process. We want each gift from God to benefit others so that He can be given glory for how we've stewarded His provision.

The final verse we'll look at is 1 Timothy 5:8: "If anyone

does not provide for his relatives, and especially for members of his household, he has denied the faith and is worse than an unbeliever." Here, Paul calls Christians to take care of those in their own household. We see the importance of this solid work ethic through the consequences of failing to live out this command—Paul says someone who doesn't do this "is worse than an unbeliever."

Let's look to Jesus as an example of what this looks like. The apostle John shares Jesus' example of how he made sure that His mother would be cared for (John 19:23-27). Ensuring that the basic needs of our immediate families are met should be a priority. After that, each married couple should pray and use wisdom from God regarding how to respond to the needs (e.g., groceries, clothes, rent or mortgage, utilities) of extended family.

These passages show us a clear biblical philosophy of stewardship: a heart that is content with all that God provides, a trust and an acknowledgment of God providing all things we're called to steward, and a desire to care for our families. And as we've already talked about, gospel-centered marriages strive to live out this stewardship philosophy within a larger rhythm of generosity.

The Dos and Don'ts of Budgeting

Elicia

Now let's get practical. Our biblical stewardship philosophy should inform us how to budget. When D. A. and I began to put together a budget, we created a list of dos and don'ts that would keep both of us accountable. This accountability structure encourages us to communicate with each other about how we spend and save. These dos and don'ts aren't commandments written in stone; rather, they're suggestions that direct our hearts to speak to each other regarding matters such as purchases, future goals, and emergency funds.

Do

Do come together to pray over your income and outflow. Be vulnerable before each other and God about financial fears, frustrations, and expectations. In prayer, acknowledge that you are not capable in your own strength to steward what God has entrusted to you. Declare your dependence on God to structure and shape the financial rhythm of your home. On your knees you will find the oneness necessary to move forward with a strategy that honors God, stewards all your financial responsibilities, and at the same time allows you to enjoy the gifts God has provided you with. If you cannot pray together over the family budget, you will likely never be on the same page.

Do make sure that you have a conversation with each other before spending money on major purchases. Each family will have their own definition of "a major purchase." In our household, a major purchase is normally anything costing more than three hundred dollars. Of course, we don't withhold communication about purchases under three hundred dollars; rather, the dollar amount simply provides a framework for a conversation. Birthday and Christmas gifts for each other are the exception. And remember, the dollar amount is not the issue— communication and compromise with your spouse is the most important thing. These conversations will allow you to walk in financial freedom, knowing that neither you nor your spouse will spend recklessly.

Do set aside time for the conversations necessary to build and adhere to the family budget.

Do define your family's financial goals. Work together to identify specific goals you want to achieve either monthly, quarterly, semiannually, or annually. In our marriage, doing this motivates D. A. and I to sacrifice certain pleasures and entertainment-driven purchases in order to put money toward the goals we set for our family. For example, three years ago we decided we wanted to open checking and savings accounts for each of our children. We first looked at our income and all our regular monthly bills and expenses, and then we determined the realistic cost of other various expenses, such as date nights and family outings. After doing these calculations, we resolved that we would set aside a certain amount every month to make deposits into our children's bank accounts. This has helped our children understand the concept of saving and spending wisely, teaching them financial stewardship with a biblical perspective at a young age. When they are older, we will give them this money for college tuition, an emergency situation, or when they are launched from our home to where God has called them to be.

Do keep a detailed expense record. If you cannot track where your money *is* going, you will have a hard time deciding where it *should* go. Since most banking is done online, many financial institutions track expenses as a courtesy. Share passwords to your individual online banking accounts (if you have separate finances) so that you and your spouse can hold each other accountable and remain on the same page regarding income and outgoing spending. And if one spouse manages the finances, providing equal access to online banking provides the other spouse a sense of security and helps him or her not to be caught off guard with income and spending. This high level of accountability can serve as a preventative tool that will keep you from fighting over finances.

Do try to avoid spending full price for clothing. There are excellent discount stores, seasonal sales, and clearance racks that offer clothes at a discounted price. I can often find clothing up to 90 percent off the original asking price!

Do remember to use coupons because the savings add up. Being a rewards member at stores can provide additional savings. We signed up at all the grocery stores in our vicinity, and sometimes, depending on the sales, we can save almost twenty dollars in a single trip!

Do put a limit on monthly recreational spending. We define recreation as entertainment, eating out, family activities, and other things of perceived value. *Perceived value* is something you and your family must work through. As human beings, we will make sacrifices for the things we find value in, sometimes to the detriment of our needs. For example, you might pay only half of the utility bill so you can use the rest of the money for a new haircut, outfit, or night out on the town. Or you'll say your budget is too tight for you to give to the local church, but you'll eat out fifteen days a month. We are more prone to fall short in financial responsibility if we don't find value in being responsible. When we don't have a balanced biblical view on finances, we will choose recreation over responsibility, with our perceived value sitting in the driver's seat.

Don't

Don't plan out a budget by yourself. The budget is for your family, and the leaders of the household should come together to discuss it.

Don't withhold any frivolous spending from your spouse. When the financial records surface and large sums of money are not accounted for, you'll face potential serious conflict and a loss of trust.

Don't open new accounts of any kind without your spouse knowing. Such practices could lead to a double life that will destroy the oneness you're trying to build together.

Don't keep all your credit cards in your phone case, purse, or wallet. We live in a day and age when smartphones actually challenge our common sense and awareness. We may not pay attention to where we place our debit or credit cards because we're responding to texts or posting something online. On more than a few occasions, both D. A. and I have misplaced our cards and have had to call the last place we made a purchase to see if we left them on the counter. When it comes to credit and debit cards—and cash—it's best to carry only what is necessary.

Don't allow extended periods of time (e.g., two or three months) to go by without sitting down together to reexamine your budget. Income streams may change (e.g., you get a raise and more can be deducted from your paycheck), and outgoing expenses may change (e.g., car insurance premiums, rent or mortgage payments). The goal is for both spouses to be on the same page to ensure a rhythm of togetherness in meeting your financial goals.

Understand Your Finances

It is vital for you and your spouse to budget together, but doing a budget, particularly if you've never done one, can be daunting. Don't be intimidated! You can do this. We encourage you to sit down with your spouse and fill in the following budget work sheet and then complete the homework assignment. The work sheet should provide a realistic assessment of your assets, streams of monthly income, and liabilities. The homework will help you and your spouse talk through your thought process on finances and how your perception may be different from reality. Having a realistic understanding of your finances and what things cost is the first step to a healthier financial climate in your home.

Exercise—The Family Budget

Assets:	
1. Savings	$
2. Checking	$
3. Real Estate Owned	$
4. Other Investments	$
Total	$

Income:	
1. Salary	$
2. Spouse's Salary	$
3. Other Income	$
Total	$

Expenses:			
1. Car Payments	$	16. Student Loans	$
2. Mortgage or Rent	$	17. College Savings	$
3. Gasoline	$	18. Property Taxes	$
4. Groceries	$	19. Personal Loans	$
5. Credit Card	$	20. Other Loans	$
6. Spouse's Credit Card	$	21. Tithes/ Offerings	$
7. Medical Bills	$	22. Eating Out	$
8. Dental Bills	$	23. Recreation	$
9. Car Insurance	$	24. Clothes	$
10. Life Insurance	$	25. Home Repairs/ Maintenance	$
11. Health Insurance	$	26. Dues/ Memberships	$
12. Renters or Homeowners Insurance	$	27. Pets	$
13. 401(k)	$	28. Babysitting	$
14. Savings	$	29. Subscriptions	$
15. Utilities	$	30. Personal Grooming	
Total $			

Homework—Go Shopping, but Don't Spend Any Money

Do you have a difficult time understanding why you're sometimes short on money? Do you think you would be a better manager of finances than your spouse? This activity will help you understand how off the mark guessing and estimations can be when it comes to budgeting. In the space provided, write down the price you think each item costs. Then, within a few days, go to the grocery store together, find these items, and price them.

	Estimated Cost	Actual Cost
1. Two cans of baked beans	$	$
2. A large box of Fruity Pebbles	$	$
3. A large box of laundry detergent	$	$
4. A five-pound bag of potatoes	$	$
5. Betty Crocker chocolate cake mix	$	$
6. A gallon of 2 percent milk	$	$
7. A medium-size jar of peanut butter	$	$

Now do the same exercise, but this time with these services and items in mind:

	Estimated Cost	Actual Cost
1. A man's haircut (+ tip)	$	$
2. A woman's haircut/style (+ tip)	$	$
3. An outfit for a woman	$	$
4. An outfit for a man	$	$
5. Sneakers for a woman	$	$
6. Sneakers for a man	$	$
7. Two tickets to the movies	$	$
8. A Bible	$	$
9. Thirteen-inch MacBook Pro	$	$

These exercises are intended to initiate a conversation between you and your spouse regarding finances, shopping, and what you can live with and without. The mock budget should show your income and outgoing expenses as well as highlight any excess. If you can't find excess in the budget, you could cut back by, for example, eating at home more often instead of at restaurants. Replacing cable with a Netflix or Hulu subscription may save money as well. Any savings could go toward your children's bank accounts or helping others who are in need. Remember, how we think about our finances should always be in the context of a culture of generosity.

Your finances don't have to put your marriage on the ropes, and they don't have to be the death of it either. In fact, gospel-saturated marriages see finances as opportunities to give God glory because any excess in the budget can help those with less. We need to trust in God, who provides all good gifts (James 1:17), and not in the gifts He gives. Imagine the impact we could have on our children, churches, and communities if we all developed a culture of generosity— enjoying the gifts God provides while meeting the needs of those around us. Perhaps people would ask about the God we worship, providing us with opportunities to share the gospel. Every action of the gospel-saturated marriage comes back to this—even something as practical as financial stewardship: We are billboards for the gospel of Jesus Christ.

CHAPTER 8

THE GOSPEL-SATURATED LIFE

You are a chosen race, a royal priesthood, a holy nation, a people
for his own possession, that you may proclaim the excellencies of
him who called you out of darkness into his marvelous light. Once
you were not a people, but now you are God's people; once you
had not received mercy, but now you have received mercy.

I PETER 2:9-10

A GOSPEL-SATURATED MARRIAGE emerges out of a gospel-saturated life, which is the high calling of all Christians. Through embracing Christ as Savior and Lord, we have been reconciled with God—and our greatest pursuit in life should be for Him. The gospel reminds us we cannot save ourselves: God Himself resurrects us out of spiritual death, making us alive with Christ (Ephesians 2:4-10). If we're living gospel-saturated lives, we're desperate for God. We will only be satisfied by remaining dependent on Him.

If we're not pursuing our relationship with Christ with everything we've got, we'll be striving for a healthy marriage in our own strength. And, as in every other area of life, relying on our own strength in marriage will cause more damage than good. We may be tempted to make marriage itself our identity—and our relationship with our spouse, not our relationship with Christ, can become our top priority. To truly live gospel-saturated lives, we need to make sure our identity is rooted in the right place.

Identity

Every Christian is a missionary, and every piece of ground we walk on is our mission field. That is our calling, married and unmarried! Our identity is not based on being married, divorced, single, or widowed—our identity is centered on the fact that we are in Christ! If we're not focusing on our identity in Christ, the everyday good and bad things of our marriages can consume us. We'll define ourselves by our spouses, depending on them for our validation and affirmation, or letting the hard aspects of marriage drag us down. If our identity is anywhere but in Christ, we'll dismiss, discount, and become discontent with God's calling to live on mission. First Peter 2:9-10 helps us understand the profound importance of our identity in Christ as we pursue a gospel-saturated life.

Don't Dismiss Your Calling

If we let anything but Christ inform our core identity, we'll be tempted to dismiss our calling. First Peter 2:9 says, "You are a chosen race, a royal priesthood, a holy nation, a people for his own possession." Every believer used to be an unbeliever—we were born in that condition (Ephesians 2:1-3)—but then we met Christ (2 Corinthians 5:17-21). Our new identity in Christ is confirmed in four ways:

1. *"A chosen race."* God has chosen us (Ephesians 1:3-6), and He is pleased with the choice He made. The people God has chosen form what Paul calls in Ephesians 2:15 the "one new man," made up of former sinners and now saints from every nation, tribe, tongue, gender, and socioeconomic status. The identity of the believer is not rooted in personal culture, ethnicity, or gender but in the fact that God chose to save us.

2. *"A royal priesthood."* A royal priesthood connects back to a bloodline of kings. The believer's identity in Christ is not a result of physical heritage, personal desire, or carnality but rather God's desire to save us (John 1:12-13). Our salvation is realized through the work of Jesus. In the Old Testament, the kings of Israel and Judah couldn't serve as priests. Uzziah attempted to and was struck with leprosy as a result (2 Chronicles 26:16-21). But 1 Peter 2:4-6 tells us that because of Christ's work, we who have been saved by Him can offer spiritual sacrifices to God. We are now both royal and a priesthood!

3. *"A holy nation."* Our identity in Christ is evidenced through our pursuit of holy living. As the Holy

Spirit matures us and we move from glory to glory (2 Corinthians 3:18), our life choices will be more in sync with His leading. Holiness will become an identifying marker in our lives as opposed to the sinfulness that used to define us.

4. *"A people for his own possession."* This phrase reminds us that this is all possible because we were purchased by the shed blood of Christ. Colossians 1:13-14 says, "He has delivered us from the domain of darkness and transferred us to the kingdom of his beloved Son, in whom we have redemption, the forgiveness of sins." We have been bought out of the slavery to sin that once held us captive. We've been forgiven of our sins, and now God sees us as covered by the righteousness of Jesus' perfect life!

These four truths should remind us that we were born outside of the family of God, but because of Jesus' shed blood (the necessary spiritual currency for purchasing us), our identity is now in Him! And we should not dismiss the profound calling that God has placed on our lives.

Don't Discount Your Calling

Knowing the incredible gift we have been given in our identity in Christ, we should express our gratitude toward our gift giver by sharing His message boldly and regularly. In the second part of verse 9, Peter says, "You may proclaim the excellencies of him who called you out of darkness into his marvelous light." God has provided us with a new identity in order to send us out to live on a mission that makes Him famous. To *proclaim* can carry the idea of modern advertising. This verb in the Greek is written in the active voice, which means the subject is required to perform the action. Every Christian is supposed to advertise the excellencies of God. God has called each member in the body of Christ to serve Him by being His marketing team! This is not a cheap calling!

Peter says that in our calling from God, we left the darkness and came into His marvelous light. God called each of us specifically by name (Romans 8:29-30; Revelation 13:8; 17:8) into His Kingdom. He's commissioned each of us in the Kingdom to live on mission by carrying out His Kingdom business. *This* is our identity—this is what informs everything we do in a gospel-saturated marriage and gospel-saturated life.

Remember your former life before coming to Christ. Ephesians 5:8 says, "At one time you were darkness, but now you are light in the Lord. Walk as children of light." Walking as children of light becomes a reality when we realize our calling is rooted in our identity in Christ.

The world is trying to woo us to place our identity in achievements, careers, education, entertainment, possessions, relationships, and so much more. Peter is telling us not to cheapen or discount our God-given calling to make Him famous. This means we get to leverage our achievements and so on as platforms for gospel proclamation and holy living.

Be excellent in the things you're gifted in doing, and do all things for the glory of God. In doing this, you'll refrain from discounting your calling and live effectively for the gospel in your life.

Don't Be Discontent with Your Calling

And last of all, as it relates to your identity, don't grow discontent in your calling. Any identity we give ourselves can easily be a place of discontent, including marriage. We can dwell on what we don't have rather than turning our eyes to what God has done for us. To fight off that temptation, consider Peter's words in verse 10: "Once you were not a people, but now you are God's people; once you had not received mercy, but now you have received mercy." Many of Peter's readers were second-class Roman citizens[1] but had full citizenship in the Kingdom of God. Their identity in Christ placed them in the family known as God's own people. He chose them to receive mercy through salvation in Jesus Christ! Did you notice all the pronouns in verse 9?

Regarding the believer's identity, "you are a chosen race" uses the second-person plural, which has a corporate reality, not singular.

Regarding the believer's calling, "you may proclaim" uses the second-person plural—again an emphasis on the corporate, not individual.

Now, the phrases "a royal priesthood," "a holy nation," and "a people for his own possession" are all singular, giving further emphasis to the one body of Christ that is called to live out one mission, together! What the enemy of our souls desires is to cause us to become discontent with our corporate identity and calling based on our individual circumstances. We mustn't grow weary in living out our calling by comparing our lives and statuses to brothers and sisters in the faith. They are our contemporaries, not our competition. We must remain faithful to the mission while living in community with our local bodies—each believer making the necessary contributions to ensure health in the lives of the body of Christ. None of these choices is dependent on being married—they're part of our common calling! This is good news!

The gospel-saturated life equips us to live as billboards for our God. The world is watching us. When people see how different we are in our communication, financial stewardship, relationships, and sexuality, they will ask us why we live the way we do. This is exactly why 1 Peter 3:15 says, "In your hearts honor Christ the Lord as holy, always being prepared to make a defense to anyone who asks you for a reason for the hope that is in you; yet do it with gentleness and respect."

When the world asks us for a reason, we get to tell them that our life's rhythm is in step with the gospel. From there, we can unpack the glorious riches of the gospel of Jesus Christ—and potentially ask individuals if they'd like to embrace Him as Savior and Lord. When we choose not

to dismiss, discount, or become discontent with the calling
He has placed on each and every one of our lives, we have
the privilege of proclaiming Him to anyone who will listen!

Go and Live It

Are you ready to join the fight for a gospel-saturated marriage? God has extended you the same grace He's given us—
grace to move beyond your brokenness and struggles and
into the light of living for Him . . . together! God the Holy
Spirit indwells you, which means that you and your spouse
can not only enter the ring but also remain in the fight and
never throw in the towel.

Your identity in Christ should compel you to live a gospel-
saturated life. And if your spouse is also a believer, you can
join together to live out a genuine gospel-saturated marriage.
Christ has already secured your victory through His resurrection. Even in the direst of circumstances in marriage, you
can hold on to this truth: God has given you the power to
reclaim your marriage for His glory. And as you do—as you
communicate well, resolve conflict biblically, walk in sexual
purity, choose financial accountability, and exemplify oneness—you can give our world a tangible illustration of the
gospel. As you live a gospel-saturated life, crucifying your
flesh and putting your faith daily in Christ (Galatians 2:20),
you can push back the darkness in your community. Will you
take this challenge? Will you embrace the gospel-saturated
marriage and life God made you for?

Come join us. It's time to enter the ring.

Epilogue

To Unmarried Christians

There is one body and one Spirit—just as you were called to the one
hope that belongs to your call—one Lord, one faith, one baptism, one
God and Father of all, who is over all and through all and in all.

EPHESIANS 4:4-6

GOSPEL-SATURATED LIVING is possible for every believer, not just for those who are married, which is why we think it's important to take a moment to speak to our unmarried brothers and sisters. According to the United States Census Bureau, in 2014, 107 million Americans who were eighteen and older were unmarried (45 percent of the population). Of these, 53 percent were women and 47 percent were men; 63 percent had never been married, 24 percent were divorced, and 13 percent were widowed. Of that 107 million, 18 million were age 65 or older.[1] To neglect the emotional, mental, physical, relational, and spiritual needs of such a substantial population is poor stewardship.

There is much that church leaders and Christian married

couples can learn from unmarried brothers and sisters. Even the term *unmarried* is one example. Although technically those of you who are unmarried may be single, not all who are unmarried have never been married. Some of you may be divorced or widowed, either with or without children. We need to consider your needs. Every believer, regardless of marital status, has a story that needs to be appreciated, heard, and valued. We want you, our unmarried brothers and sisters, to feel embraced and understood.

Our Humble Approach

Before we jump in, we want to acknowledge a few limitations on our end. We married young—in our early twenties—and never lived on our own before we got married. With this in mind, neither of us is going to act as though we know what it means to live as a Christian who is divorced, never married, or widowed. We've been transparent throughout this entire book, so we're not going to start frontin' now.

Next, we want to express heartfelt appreciation to all our unmarried brothers and sisters who have spent countless hours sharing their stories with us over these past ten years as we've served as leaders in the local church. We have drunk deeply from your wells of wisdom and have gained a greater devotion to seeing the unmarried believer celebrated and included in the family of God, local church, and overall global mission. Although we can't identify with your every struggle, we can empathize with you as believers who are being progressively sanctified daily. Our hearts are for you, and we desire the privilege of encouraging you in your faith as you engage in fighting the same worldly system as your married brothers and sisters in Christ.

We want these words to be read with an Ephesians 4:29 perspective—that our conversation with you would be a blessing to others. As we speak with you, our hope is that our married brothers and sisters are edified and given insight for action. We long to see the interpersonal relationships of the entire body of Christ improved as we come together to meet one another's needs.

Unmarried brothers and sisters, first allow us grace to affirm your value! We view you as spiritual warriors in the army of God, equally colaboring on the front lines in the body of Christ's spiritual war. The body needs your vantage point, voice, and vocation to reach the lost and produce disciples. We know you may have experienced wounds within the church, and we want to speak life to those wounds. We have a few goals: to acknowledge the *giftedness* of your status, provide a biblical framework for it, and challenge our Christian leaders (and married couples) in local churches to create spaces of communal inclusion for you.

You're Not Second-Class Citizens

D. A.

We often hear unmarried believers of various ages express frustration about the lack of space for them in the local church. Many feel that the "singles ministry" in their church is like

Youth Group 2.0 or College Group Part 2. The content of teaching lacks biblical and practical depth. Church events, sermon illustrations, and the overall rhythm of church life seem directed more toward married couples and families. Many of our unmarried brothers and sisters wrestle with thoughts of being second-class citizens in the Kingdom of God!

To all our unmarried family members, please know this couldn't be further from the truth. We know from Scripture that God the Holy Spirit does not indwell married saints in a greater capacity than those who are unmarried. The gospel message does not declare that unmarried people receive a discounted payment for their sins.

On behalf of church leaders and married Christians on this side of eternity, we want to offer you a heartfelt apology. We apologize for not including you more; for pigeonholing you to volunteer in ministries you feel profile your unmarried status; and for assuming that since you're not married, you have more than 24 hours in a day, 7 days in a week, and 365 days in a year to live on mission. These misunderstandings have created feelings of abandonment, isolation, and neglect, causing you to feel like stepchildren in the body of Christ.

We want to walk in repentance by loving you in word and deed. The greatest way we can express our love to you is by telling you that you are not second-class citizens in the Kingdom of God. Being unmarried does not remove your need for sound doctrine, quality shepherding, and opportunities to use your spiritual gifts to edify saints in your local churches. You are equal participants in the great commandment, great commission, and great commitment. Since there is equality for all saints in Christ (Galatians 3:28), we want to fight for equity in meeting your needs with the same passion and vigor as we do for all other saints in Christ's body.

Consider also the words of Paul in 1 Corinthians 7 and how he has much to say regarding your status being a gift and how you can steward this gift. In verse 7 Paul says, "I wish that all were as I myself am. But each has his own gift from God, one of one kind and one of another." Paul admits in the next verse he was unmarried when he wrote this epistle.

Marriage is not a prerequisite for being used by God to edify your brothers and sisters in Christ, including those who are married. You have unique contributions to offer through your life experience, biblical knowledge, and ministry expertise in areas beyond babysitting or serving as youth workers or Sunday school teachers. The truth in Scripture you mine during your personal devotion time can, and should, strengthen the spiritual walks of all those sitting around the table you've been invited to. We pray that you receive more invitations to share meals with married couples and that when you do, you contribute the things that are simmering in your hearts.

Paul also said each person's status is a gift. In this context, the word *gift* means God-given generosity to find contentment in sexual matters.[2] Although there are different statuses for the unmarried—divorced, never married, and widowed—Paul's wording provides each unmarried person with the comfort and truth that God has given him or her grace for a specific season. This grace allows them not only to mature during this season of life but also to participate in communal life in the body of Christ.

Gleaning from Paul's first letter to the Corinthians, here are some benefits of this grace, which is available to all in Christ, married and unmarried alike: boasting in the work of Christ (1:28-30); holding other members in the body accountable (chapter 5); running from sexual immorality (6:12-20); walking in wisdom regarding Christian liberties (chapter 8); fleeing idolatry while doing all things in life for God's glory (chapter 10); and participating in the Lord's Supper (11:17-34). This grace also includes edifying the body of Christ through spiritual gifts (12:1-11); embodying the love of God (chapter 13); participating in orderly worship (14:26-40); defending the faith by proclaiming the gospel while walking in assurance because of the Resurrection (chapter 15); and helping those in need (16:1-4).

All of this to say, no matter your age or status, whether you're loving the unmarried state or lonely because of it, God has not forsaken you. His grace for you will never run out. Married couples in the body of Christ need to be running alongside you (and you them) during this marathon of the faith we're enduring together (Hebrews 12:1-2).

Now, before you assume all the things we're saying are romantic and unrealistic, let's consider what Paul says in 1 Corinthians 7:8-9: "I say to those who aren't married and to widows—it's better to stay unmarried, just as I am. But if they can't control themselves, they should go ahead and marry. It's better to marry than to burn with lust" (NLT).

Yeah, Paul just got real. Let's not be so naive regarding the desire for sexual intimacy and pleasure while being unmarried. God created sexual intimacy as a gift, and it's tough to abstain when you're desiring sex. Sometimes you may be tempted and put yourself in a situation where your goal for the evening is to have sex, while other times someone has pursued you and you give in for a moment's pleasure.

This is where authentic accountability and biblical counsel are necessary. Paul says it's "better to marry than to burn with lust"; however, we know that marrying just to have sex is not healthy. Marriage is not the cure for lust, so getting married and assuming that your burning desire for sex will go away is unrealistic. This is why Paul makes the appeal regarding self-control. If an unmarried person is wrestling with lust but is able to remain pure, Paul says, stay unmarried in order to avoid "worldly troubles" (1 Corinthians 7:28). Paul unpacks what he means in verses 32-38: Married people face a different set of challenges, namely "family responsibilities,"[3] that may put limitations on living on mission.

In the same line of thinking, many unmarried people know such limitations because they, too, are blessed to have children. Their availability for going on mission trips, serving in multiple ministries, and fellowshiping a few nights a week should be regulated based on the needs of their children. After all, their children are their first ministry, not the programs their church offers.

We want to talk about one more misconception here: that the unmarried person has more time for ministry. Sure, unmarried people may not have spousal responsibilities and some may not be parents, but many are knee-deep in their careers, have hobbies, are involved in various forms of outreach, or leverage their time serving others. They can be just as strapped for time as married believers, often due to being involved in fellowship, school, or ministries in the church after they get off work. The best way to dispel this misunderstanding in the church is for the married and unmarried to spend time together, perhaps over meals, talking through commitments, brainstorming about how to offer mutual support, and fanning the flames of passion in areas of special interest.

Elicia and I have benefited greatly from our relationships with unmarried brothers and sisters. Some of the unmarried sisters in our local church lent us their expertise and wisdom when we were struggling with our son Duce's speech delay. They had come over for dinner other times, but this time they schooled us during dessert.

Their counsel was comforting and timely, and we didn't take it with a grain of salt simply because they're not mothers! No—we affirmed their skill sets, education, and training and let them know we would follow their advice.

This is one simple way of affirming the unmarried: inviting them into community, allowing them to provide counsel and wisdom—and not pressuring them about getting married, asking why they're still single, or trying to hook them up on blind dates. If the words of Paul express the unmarried status as a gift from God, where contentment and mission are tangible realities, we should echo this to our unmarried brothers and sisters.

If our unmarried brothers and sisters do indeed express a desire to be married, we must not automatically turn into matchmakers who seek to hook them up with every prospect we come across. We should affirm that their desire to be married is not sinful (1 Corinthians 7:9, 28) and at the same time ask them for grace, as married couples, to walk alongside them through the process of praying for a spouse as they remain pure until the Lord answers favorably. We should desire to protect the hearts of our unmarried brothers and sisters who long for marriage. Sometimes, infatuation and longing for *the one* can blind a person to the dangers others may see.

This is why gospel-saturated marriages are necessary in local churches: They provide those who desire to get married with a picture of two broken people who have both entrusted their hearts to God (through salvation in Jesus Christ) and each other while living in a broken world that keeps trying to break them apart.

A gospel-saturated marriage puts its blemishes on display so onlookers can see the present tense work of God. This will help the unmarried who desire marriage to not allow the idea of *marriage* to replace Jesus on the throne of their hearts.

Purity in Relationships
One struggle that unmarried brothers and sisters have shared with us is that few sermons speak directly to their reality. There

are plenty of sermons, illustrations, and applications that deal with marriage and family, but application for unmarried people tends to be limited to general sweeping statements.

Therefore, we're devoting a section to purity in relationships—not because we think unmarried people are the only believers called to purity but because we want to honor you by digging into what this looks like in your current situation. The complexities of how to remain pure while living in community with other believers is rarely, if ever, touched on by a full sermon. We typically receive five common questions from unmarried believers who desire marriage but want clarity on navigating through this tension.

1. How is an unmarried believer who desires to be married supposed to live?

We are made in the image of God (Genesis 1:26-27), and this means that our desire to love someone of the opposite gender and have a committed relationship with him or her comes from God, and it is both natural and healthy. It is not wrong to desire to be married, just as it is not wrong to be unmarried and *not* desire marriage. In Scripture we see two common relationships between men and women: brothers and sisters (1 Timothy 5:1-2) and married couples (Ephesians 5:22-23).

We challenge our unmarried brothers and sisters to view God as their primary source of love, since He was the only one who demonstrated His love for us while we were unbelievers (John 3:16; Romans 5:8). Because God loves us perfectly, we should look to Him to fulfill the longings in our hearts. For some, this means trusting Him to supply the spouse He desires, in the timing He desires (Genesis 2:18, 24). As Proverbs 19:14 says, "House and wealth are inherited from fathers, but a prudent wife is from the LORD." For others, He gives a unique measure of grace and giftedness as He calls and designs them for singleness (Jeremiah 16:2; 1 Corinthians 7:7). In the body of Christ, we must respect God's calling on each person and entrust the Lord to lead him or her as He desires.

All unmarried believers must strive to live on mission for His glory. Living on mission in community will provide the framework necessary for fellowship and holy living. Community will safeguard you from trying to walk in purity while in isolation. Isolation leads us toward condemning ourselves when we fall into sin rather than running to the cross and the community of faith for grace, hope, and spiritual restoration (Galatians 6:1-2).

2. How will I know if he or she is "the one"?

This is a much-debated question. Some people believe there's no one person for any of us but rather a certain type of person. Others believe there is only one person for each individual. We encourage you not to focus on "the one" but instead to evaluate the character of a potential spouse. We've provided the following questions to help you:

- Does he or she show evidence of a personal walk with God (John 10:27; Romans 8:14-16; 10:9-10; 1 John 3:3, 14; 4:6)?

- Have you known this person long enough to become attracted to him or her holistically? Have you been able to assess this individual's commitment to Christ and His church; a pattern of integrity; emotional intellect; physical attractiveness; personality chemistry; and the calling from God on his or her life (Ephesians 4–6; Colossians 3:1-17; 2 Peter 1:5-7)?

- What are practical ways you both will work in harmony to fulfill God's calling on your lives?

- Does this person share the same desire to be with you as you have for him or her?

- How can your church leadership walk you through the process of entering the covenant of marriage?

These questions take time to answer. One key part of discerning someone's character is spending time with him or her in community as well as one-on-one. Your family, local church leadership, and holistic discipleship team should be able to see how you and this person react to life situations in the moment: holiday gatherings, church functions, meals in homes with friends, and dates in public venues. You'll be able to see the multifaceted vantage points of the person's character while dealing with everyday life issues such as traffic, long admission lines, and relational conflict.

Over the course of time, the filters we humans put on our actions and words fall away because we become more comfortable around others. It's during these times that those close to you need to assess both you and the person you may marry. Your close community will know if you're being superficial or genuine, and they'll be able to see how your potential partner treats you in light of your actions.

Your church leadership and holistic discipleship team are there to help you pump the brakes before you rush into marriage or to help you realize that you are ready to enter into the covenant of marriage.

3. How will I know it's the right time for marriage?

This subjective question is regularly met with a diversity of answers: "No one is ever ready"; "Wait until after you get your degree"; "Wait until you're five years into your career." Discerning the right timing is really discerning the will of God (which we'll discuss in the next section), and this is best done in community with your local pastor (or church leadership) and holistic discipleship team. However, we do want to provide a suggested framework for discerning where you are in your relationship. When we've provided counsel to unmarried couples, we've asked them to identify where they are in their relationship and where they desire to go. Here are the five stages of relationship:

Brother and sister in Christ: Friends who both identify Jesus Christ as their Lord and Savior. At this stage, contact is exclusive to group functions. There are no individual emotional, physical, or spiritual deposits being made at this level. Most relationships stay at this level; however, if one or both people desire to get to know the other beyond this level, he or she will express that desire, share a phone number, or suggest plans for exclusive time together.

Dating: This label is often a cause of division in Christian circles. We do not recommend this term for children or young teenagers. However, if unmarried brothers and sisters are older and have a holistic discipleship team in place, they have the guidance and accountability needed for remaining pure at this level. When unmarried brothers and sisters tell us they're going out on a date, they're simply calling it what it is, so we will use that term to identify this level of relationship. At this level it's best to have a balance of dates together and including others (double dates or group dates).

A group setting is preferable for an initial date, especially if there's been no established friendship. During times out, focus on getting to know the person socially (group dates, fellowship events) and, in a limited way, spiritually (asking questions about his or her personal beliefs, convictions, and so on). Take note of how he or she interacts with others (friends, church family). Maintain sexual purity by practicing 1 Thessalonians 4:3-5: "This is the will of God, your sanctification: that you abstain from sexual immorality; that each one of you know how to control his own body in holiness and honor, not in the passion of lust like the Gentiles who do not know God."

Courting: At this level, the man and woman have agreed to be exclusive, meaning they are not seeking any other dating or courting relationships. If you are at this level, you and your church leadership and holistic discipleship team understand that this person is a serious prospect for marriage, and you are both seeking accountability regarding whether to pursue engagement. Having conversations about Scripture, God's calling on your lives, career paths, and life rhythm is important—you will have direction on how to pray, and you'll know if God is drawing you toward marriage. If you both sense a green light and receive affirmation from those you're in community with, engagement is the next step. Maintain sexual purity.

Engagement: Here, you and the other person make a formal commitment. Continue to develop your social relationships. With wisdom, pursue spiritual interaction (Bible study, prayer, and so on) because now is the time to begin digging into the Word and having regular devotions together! Maintain serious physical standards and set limits on possible physical contact—you're not married, and during this stage, things can still be broken off, so don't fall into regular times of physical affection. Because marriage is not yet a reality, continue to adhere to 1 Thessalonians 4:3-5.

Marriage: This is a lifetime commitment. Feel free to go back and read through chapters 1 through 7 of this book together. Remember, don't just date to marry—marry to date! Continue to make the time to go out on dates together; invest in each other.

Without labels in relationships, there is ambiguity, and people's hearts get broken too easily. Now, demanding a label for the sake of security can be just as damaging; being too aggressive may come off as needy and desperate. In light of this, we suggest seeking a label if exclusive time together on the phone (including texting) and going out is becoming normal. If there are emotional investments being made (e.g., purchasing sentimental gifts, daily communication, scheduled dates), it's time to label what you have and then discuss if you should pursue a future pathway (maintaining the wise counsel of church leadership and your holistic discipleship team).

4. What is an acceptable sex life for the unmarried believer?

Every believer, regardless of his or her status, is called to live a life of sexual purity. As we talked about earlier in this book, we are all to pursue purity both before and after marriage.

Sex is a beautiful gift from God to humanity. The framework in which God desires this gift to be enjoyed is within the boundaries of marriage between one man and one woman. We fully understand that many may disagree with us; however, this is our biblical conviction. Stating this creates space for us to hold our ground while respecting those who disagree with us and desiring to engage in continued conversation with them.

Regarding the question of an acceptable sex life for the unmarried believer, we must say that all sexual activity outside of marriage, as God defines it, is sinful. In 1 Corinthians 6:18, Paul instructs believers to "flee from sexual immorality." The Greek word Paul uses for "sexual immorality" is *porneia*, which can include any sexual activity outside of the framework God has set. Sexual immorality of every kind is condemned in Scripture;[4] it's never accepted, championed, or overlooked.

The word Paul uses to describe sexual relations was often used to describe the lighting of a fire.[6] The boundaries for abstinence for the unmarried are similar to those in place for a fire in a fireplace. If someone wants to start a fire, the flue must be opened and the logs and kindling must be set; however, without a spark or flame, the fire won't burn. When the fire is ignited, it burns beautifully, providing warmth and light. As long as the fire remains in the fireplace, it's fulfilling its intended purpose. If it gets outside of its boundaries, it destroys everything in its path until it has either burned out or is put out.

In a similar way, the God-given boundary for sex (fire) is marriage (the fireplace). Since humans are sexual beings, we already have every component necessary for a fire, but outside of marriage we're not within the fireplace. If we put ourselves in a position where we allow another person to light our fire outside of marriage, holistic danger—emotional, mental, physical, and spiritual—may result. The potential destruction includes emotional baggage, mental stress, a loss of purity, and possible physical issues ranging from disease to pregnancy.

This is why Paul says that abstaining from sexual immorality is the best safeguard. Like us, he lived in a sexually charged world, and yet he still provided this counsel. It is possible for any unmarried Christian, regardless of age, to keep this command. "Possible" doesn't mean easy, though, which is why it's necessary to walk in community with other believers who can hold you accountable (and vice versa).

5. How do I move forward from the guilt of my past sins?

The gospel speaks to all our sin, including sexual sin. If we have embraced Christ as our Savior, He's provided forgiveness for our sins and bought us out of slavery (Ephesians 1:7, Romans 6:6), and we no longer have to obey our sinful desires (Romans 6:1-14). It's crucial for those who've had a sexually sinful past to not feel as if they're damaged goods, unworthy to be loved, or second-class citizens in the Kingdom of God.

When it comes to the sinful choices of your past, you can move forward just as every other believer can. These four Cs can remind you of your positional reality in Christ:

Christ paid the penalty for your sins (Romans 5:8; 1 Peter 3:18).

Christ's death cleansed you from the guilt and penalty for sin (Romans 8:31-39; 1 Corinthians 6:9-11; Acts 22:16; Ephesians 5:25-27).

Confession to God provides His forgiveness (1 John 1:8-10).

Community will help you fight for purity (Galatians 6:1-2).

Remember, the gospel-saturated life empowers every believer to apply the gospel to all areas of life, including sexual encounters. Condemnation comes from only one source: the enemy of your soul (Romans 8:1). If you follow Christ, you are walking in forgiveness. As you walk forward in sexual purity and forgiveness, God will use any mess in your past as a message of comfort to your brothers and sisters who are struggling in their fight for purity (2 Corinthians 1:3-7; Galatians 6:1-2).

We encourage you to critically think through how you'll fight for purity in your thoughts, relationships, potential engagement, and marriage. Be proactive in doing so! Ask yourself questions regarding your *thought life* (What will I allow and not allow my mind to dwell on?), *dating* (What are my standards for investments of time in a relationship that may not lead to courting or engagement?), *engagement* (What are the sexual standards we will live out before we take our vows?), and *marriage* (How will my spouse and I pursue purity for the remainder of our lives?). Develop a biblical philosophy for each of the areas and share them with those you're in discipleship relationships with.

We Are the Church

Many unmarried believers have experienced seasons of isolation and loneliness, and our hearts grieve with theirs.

It's imperative for the local church to create space for our unmarried brothers and sisters. We can do so by inviting them to live life with us outside of church functions; walking in gender-specific meaningful discipleship relationships together; and considering their differing needs based on age. (Unmarried believers in their twenties have different sets of needs than those in their forties—but you can't seek to meet the needs of unmarried believers you've never taken the time to meet and get to know.)

Married believers must also fight off the urge to show pity by attempting to hook up unmarried believers. We must refrain from doing this especially if we do not have a meaningful relationship with them or their permission!

The entire church must affirm the value of our unmarried brothers and sisters, and those who are married can do this by engaging with them in regular gospel-saturated conversations. We're all fighting off the same worldly system together, and we as the body of Christ must be unified. When one is hurting or doubting their value, may we rush to them and remind them of their identity in Christ. As we do this, we're empowering them to walk with us as we pursue purity in our relationships. We're all equal citizens in the Kingdom of God—a family—and we must begin to embody this reality as a testimony to the watching world.

Notes

CHAPTER 1: BEAT THE WORLD TO THE PUNCH

1. See, for example, Adam Liptak, "Supreme Court Ruling Makes Same-Sex Marriage a Right Nationwide," *New York Times*, June 26, 2015, https://www.nytimes.com/2015/06/27/us/supreme-court-same-sex-marriage.html?_r=0.
2. See, for example, Aaron Earls, "Christian Twitter Reaction to Gay Marriage Ruling," *The Wardrobe Door* (blog), June 26, 2015, http://thewardrobedoor.com/2015/06/christian-twitter-reaction-to-gay-marriage-ruling.html.
3. William Arndt, Frederick W. Danker, and Walter Bauer, *A Greek-English Lexicon of the New Testament and Other Early Christian Literature*, 3rd ed. (Chicago: University of Chicago Press, 2000), 879.
4. See Henry Jackson Flanders, Jr., "Marriage in the New Testament," in Watson E. Mills, ed., *Mercer Dictionary of the Bible* (Macon, GA: Mercer University Press, 1990), 553. Flanders says, "The Bible opens and closes with a marital union concept."
5. Andreas Kostenberger, "The Bible's Teaching on Marriage and Family," Family Research Council, accessed November 1, 2016, http://www.frc.org/brochure/the-bibles-teaching-on-marriage-and-family.
6. William J. Duiker and Jackson J. Spielvogel, *World History*, 7th ed. (Boston: Wadsworth, 2013), 13.
7. George P. Monger, *Marriage Customs of the World: From Henna to Honeymoons* (Santa Barbara, CA: ABC-Clio, 2004), 194.
8. Karen K. Hersch, *The Roman Wedding: Ritual and Meaning in Antiquity* (New York: Cambridge University Press, 2010), 20.
9. Monger, *Marriage Customs*, 194.
10. Steven Leonard Jacobs, *The Jewish Experience: An Introduction to Jewish History and Jewish Life* (Minneapolis: Fortress Press, 2010), 156.

11. Bruce K. Waltke with Cathi J. Fredricks, *Genesis: A Commentary* (Grand Rapids, MI: Zondervan, 2001), 88.

12. See Alfred Edersheim, *Sketches of Jewish Social Life in the Days of Christ* (London: Religious Tract Society, 1876), 60, and Matthew Henry, *Matthew Henry's Commentary on the Whole Bible*, New Modern Edition (Peabody, MA: Hendrickson, 1994), Logos Bible Software: Genesis 2:21-25.

13. *Macmillan Dictionary*, s.v. "consummation," accessed August 9, 2017, http://www.macmillandictionary.com/us/dictionary/american/consummation.

14. H. D. M. Spence-Jones, ed., *The Pulpit Commentary: Genesis*, vol. 1 (New York: Funk & Wagnalls Company, 1909), 53.

15. James Swanson, *A Dictionary of Biblical Languages with Semantic Domains: Hebrew (Old Testament)* (Oak Harbor, WA: Logos Research Systems, 2001), Logos Bible Software, 1815.

CHAPTER 3: CAN WE TALK?

1. Pastor David T. Moore, "He Said, She Said . . . ," from the second sermon in his series "Love for a Lifetime," How Marriage Works.com, accessed November 16, 2016, https://howmarriageworks.com/heshe.php.

2. Jud Wilhite, *That Crazy Little Thing Called Love: The Soundtrack of Marriage, Sex, and Faith* (Cincinnati: Standard, 2007), 35.

3. Kira S. Birditt et al., eds., "Marital Conflict Behaviors and Implications for Divorce Over 16 Years," *Journal of Marriage and Family* 72 (October 2010): 1188–204, doi:10.1111/j.1741-3737.2010.00758.x.

4. Ellie Lisitsa, "The Four Horsemen: Criticism, Contempt, Defensiveness, and Stonewalling," *The Gottman Relationship Blog*, April 24, 2013, https://www.gottman.com/blog/the-four-horsemen-recognizing-criticism-contempt-defensiveness-and-stonewalling/.

5. John Gray, *Men Are from Mars, Women Are from Venus: The Definitive Guide to Relationships* (London: Element, 1992), 155.

6. John Powell, *Why Am I Afraid to Tell You Who I Am?* (Grand Rapids, MI: Zondervan, 1999), 30–36.

7. Gary Chapman, "Mastering Your Spouse's Love Language," Focus on the Family, accessed November 1, 2016, http://www.focusonthefamily.com/marriage/communication-and-conflict/mastering-your-spouses-love-language.

8. Gary Chapman, *The Five Love Languages: The Secret to Love That Lasts* (Chicago: Northfield Publishing, 2015).

9. Amanda Lenhart and Maeve Duggan, "Couples, the Internet, and Social Media: How American Couples Use Digital Technology to Manage Life,

Logistics, and Emotional Intimacy within Their Relationships," Pew Research Center, February 11, 2014, http://www.pewinternet.org/2014 /02/11/couples-the-internet-and-social-media/.

CHAPTER 4: GOING THE DISTANCE

1. *Merriam-Webster's Dictionary*, s.v. "machismo," https://www.merriam -webster.com/dictionary/machismo. This word, meaning "a strong sense of masculine pride: an exaggerated masculinity," has positive and negative connotations in Chicano culture, which leads to my qualification of how I'm using it. In context, I'm speaking of the sense of pride I wrestle with as a man. This sense of pride doesn't want me to listen to the advice and counsel of my wife or children, let alone allow them to see me in a state of vulnerability. The Chicano (male) struggle with exhibiting machismo is real; yet when we are indwelled by God the Holy Spirit, we must realize He is greater than our sense of pride. My use of *machismo* captured the struggle of trying to be strong before my wife and kids by not allowing them to see how the death of my cousin affected me. My weeping and weakness highlighted the strength of God who carries me when I feel as though I can't go on.

CHAPTER 5: IT STARTS AT HOME

1. For insights regarding the Malaysian expression of this, see A. Scott Loveless and Thomas B. Holman, eds., *The Family in the New Millennium: Strengthening the Family* (Westport, CT: Praeger, 2007), 181–91; regarding Chinese society, see G. William Skinner, ed., *The Study of Chinese Society: Essays by Maurice Freedman* (Stanford, CA: Stanford University Press, 1979), 240–54; and regarding Mexican cultural structure see Larissa Adler Lomnitz, *The Family on the Threshold of the 21st Century: Trends and Implications*, ed. Solly Dreman (Mahwah, NJ: Lawrence Erlbaum Associates, 1997), 113–24: chapter 7: "Family, Networks, and Survival on the Threshold of the 21st Century in Urban Mexico."

2. *Merriam-Webster's Collegiate Dictionary*, 11th ed., s.v. "productive," https:// www.merriam-webster.com/dictionary/productive.

3. Dr. Greg Popcak, "Losing My Religion: Why People are REALLY Leaving the Church (It's Not What You Think)," *Faith on the Couch* (blog), Patheos, May 12, 2015, http://www.patheos.com/blogs/faithonthecouch/2015/05 /losing-my-religion-why-people-are-really-leaving-the-church-its-not-what -you-think/.

4. "Nearly 6 Out of 10 Children Participate in Extracurricular Activities, Census Bureau Reports," United States Census Bureau, December 9, 2014, http://www.census.gov/newsroom/press-releases/2014/cb14-224.html.

5. Sarah Eekhoff Zylstra, "Ben Zobrist: Major League Believer," The Gospel Coalition, October 18, 2016, https://www.thegospelcoalition.org/article /ben-zobrist-major-league-believer.

6. Marc Prensky, "Digital Natives, Digital Immigrants Part 1," *On the Horizon* 9, no. 5 (October 2001):1, MCB University Press, http:// www.marcprensky.com/writing/Prensky%20-%20Digital%20Natives ,%20Digital%20Immigrants%20-%20Part1.pdf.

7. You can log on to dkit.uywi.org, register to become a user for free, and have access to all the content we offer at UYWI for the discipleship of digital natives. You can even track the growth of your disciples and provide us with feedback and reports on how they're responding to the material. The idea behind this toolkit is simple—it does not produce disciples; the parents and youth workers do. UYWI exists to resource parents and youth workers with tools that can help them make disciples.

CHAPTER 6: CAN WE STAY PURE?

1. Craig S. Keener, *1–2 Corinthians* (New York: Cambridge University Press, 2005), 62–63. As it relates to "having" one's own husband/wife, Craig Keener says this phrase is synonymous with a person having another person sexually, meaning a sexually intimate encounter. This is to be understood as a monogamous relationship between a husband and wife.

2. William Arndt, Frederick W. Danker, and Walter Bauer, *A Greek-English Lexicon of the New Testament and Other Early Christian Literature*, 3rd ed. (Chicago: University of Chicago Press, 2000), 54.

3. James Swanson, *A Dictionary of Biblical Languages with Semantic Domains: Greek (New Testament)* (Oak Harbor, WA: Logos Research Systems, 1997), 299.

4. Paul Ellingworth, *The Epistle to the Hebrews: A Commentary on the Greek Text* (Grand Rapids, MI: Eerdmans, 1993), 697.

5. Luke Gilkerson, "Resources for Women Who Struggle with Porn," Covenant Eyes, June 30, 2014, http://www.covenanteyes.com/2014/06 /30/resources-women-struggle-porn/.

6. Thomas L. Constable, "Notes on Matthew: 2017 Edition," Sonic Light, 111, http://www.soniclight.org/constable/notes/pdf/matthew.pdf.

7. Luke Gilkerson, "3 Gospel Principles for Battling Porn Addiction," Covenant Eyes, August 8, 2014, http://www.covenanteyes.com/2014/08 /08/battling-porn-addiction/.

8. Paul Maxwell, "Seven Things to Do After You Look at Pornography," Desiring God, March 9, 2016, http://www.desiringgod.org/articles/seven -things-to-do-after-you-look-at-pornography.

9. Andraé Crouch, "The Blood Will Never Lose Its Power," *Take the Message Everywhere* (Sony/ATV Music, 1970).

CHAPTER 7: ON THE ROPES

1. Kelley Holland, "Fighting with Your Spouse? It's Probably about This," CNBC, February 4, 2015, http://www.cnbc.com/2015/02/04/money-is -the-leading-cause-of-stress-in-relationships.html.
2. "Divorce Study: Financial Arguments Early in Relationship May Predict Divorce," *HuffPost*, last modified July 16, 2013, http://www .huffingtonpost.com/2013/07/12/divorce-study_n_3587811.html.
3. "Love and Money: People Say They Save, Partner Spends, According to SunTrust Survey," SunTrust, February 4, 2015, http://investors .suntrust.com/news/news-details/2015/Love-and-Money-People-Say -They-Save-Partner-Spends-According-to-SunTrust-Survey/default.aspx.
4. To learn more about the Multiply initiative, see "Multiply Two-Year Goals," The Summit Church, http://www.summitrdu.com/multiply /about/. And to review the initial sermon series, see "Fall 2016 Multiply Resources," The Summit Church, http://www.summitrdu.com/multiply /resources/#1478613463679-a642d421-0628. Also check out J. D. Greear, *Gaining by Losing: Why the Future Belongs to Churches That Send* (Grand Rapids, MI: Zondervan, 2015). This book sets up the framework for truly living a lifestyle of generosity.
5. The content pertaining to the Generosity Matrix is from notes I took at J. D. Greear's presentation for the Summit Network residents on December 7, 2015.
6. Thomas L. Constable, "Notes on Matthew: 2017 Edition," Sonic Light, 138, http://www.soniclight.org/constable/notes/pdf/matthew.pdf.

CHAPTER 8: THE GOSPEL-SATURATED LIFE

1. Scot McKnight, *1 Peter: The NIV Application Commentary* (Grand Rapids, MI: Zondervan, 1996), 150–55.

EPILOGUE: TO UNMARRIED CHRISTIANS

1. "FFF: Unmarried and Single Americans Week Sept. 20–26, 2015," United States Census Bureau, September 15, 2015, http://www.census .gov/newsroom/facts-for-features/2015/cb15-ff19.html.
2. William Arndt, Frederick W. Danker, and Walter Bauer, *A Greek-English Lexicon of the New Testament and Other Early Christian Literature*, 3rd ed. (Chicago: University of Chicago Press, 2000), 1081.
3. Dr. Thomas Constable says, "Comparing two equally committed Christians,

an 'unmarried' man can give more concentrated attention to 'the things of the Lord.' A 'married' man needs to also be concerned about his family responsibilities. This is true of women, . . . as well as men." Thomas L. Constable, "Notes on 1 Corinthians: 2017 Edition," Sonic Light, 101, http://www.soniclight.org/constable/notes/pdf/1corinthians.pdf.

4. Some of the passages we identify condemning sexual immorality are: Genesis 19; Leviticus 18; 20; Matthew 15:19; Mark 7:21; John 8:41; Acts 15:20, 29; 21:25; Romans 1:26-29; 1 Corinthians 6:9-10, 13-18; 10:8; 2 Corinthians 12:21; Galatians 5:19; Ephesians 5:3; Colossians 3:5; 1 Thessalonians 4:3; 1 Timothy 1:10; Revelation 2:14, 20-21; 9:21; 14:8; 17:2; 18:3, 9; 19:2.

5. Richard L. Pratt Jr., *I & II Corinthians,* vol. 7 of *Holman New Testament Commentary,* ed. Max Anders (Nashville: B&H, 2000), 112.

6. See Arndt, Danker, and Bauer, *A Greek-English Lexicon,* 126; also see James Swanson, *Dictionary of Biblical Languages with Semantic Domains: Greek (New Testament)* (Oak Harbor, WA: Logos Research Systems, 1997).

BREAK FREE

*from the performance trap and
be captured by grace.*

Escaping Performance

BOUND TO BE FREE

to Be Captured by Grace

D. A. HORTON

THERE IS HOPE. THERE IS FREEDOM. IT'S TIME TO BREAK FREE
FROM THE PERFORMANCE TRAP AND REST IN THE
GLORIOUS CAPTIVITY OF GOD'S GRACE.

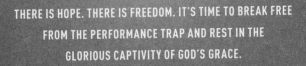

NAVPRESS

CP1123